Adam [illegible] 2012 and very quickl[illegible]on. His straight-talking [illegible]onsense attitude has wo[illegible].

In D[illegible] Norfolk (actually, Evan called on Adam to help him with his dog) and one thing led to another. Between them they decided to partner up and develop an online training platform that now has more than 3.5 million followers and 12,000 members worldwide.

Also by Adam Spivey

How to Raise the Perfect Dog

ADAM SPIVEY
OF SOUTHEND DOG TRAINING

HOW TO TRAIN YOUR DOG

ROBINSON

ROBINSON

First published in Great Britain in 2023
by Southend Dog Training Ltd

This edition published in 2023 by
Robinson

10 9 8 7 6

A CIP catalogue record for this book is available from the British Library.

ISBN: 978-1-47214-858-2

Typeset in Sentinel by
SX Composing DTP, Rayleigh, Essex
Printed and bound in Great Britain by
Clays Ltd, Elcograf S.p.A.

Papers used by Robinson are from well-managed forests and other responsible sources.

MIX
Supporting responsible forestry
FSC® C104740

Robinson
An imprint of
Little, Brown Book Group
Carmelite House
50 Victoria Embankment
London EC4Y 0DZ
An Hachette UK Company

www.hachette.co.uk

www.littlebrown.co.uk

This book is dedicated to our followers and our team, because without everyone's support none of this would be possible.

Contents

Introduction

Hey guys, what's going on? Adam Spivey here, founder and director of Southend Dog Training (SDT). I've been training dogs now for more than ten years and, alongside my business partner Evan Norfolk, have built SDT into one of the most successful dog training companies in the world, with a social media following of over 3.5 million.

First up, a quick thank you for buying the book, it's a great step towards a better relationship with your dog and enjoying your lives together over the years to come. You're here because you love your pet and you want to improve the bond you share going forward, ironing out any of the difficulties you might be experiencing. We can do that together.

Everything we do at SDT is no-bullshit and straight to the point. We offer easy-to-follow advice that everyone can work with to help their dog, regardless of its breed or problem. SDT has helped all sorts of dogs and all sorts of owners from all over the place. Our advice is suitable for all dog breeds, mixes and sizes, and for all people, regardless of age, gender or lifestyle. We've got things sorted for first-time owners with boisterous puppies and families struggling with training their older pets, to experienced handlers working with nervous rescue dogs that everyone else has given up on. Whatever your circumstances, SDT is here for you.

My passion for establishing a top-quality training programme for dogs comes from my own experience. Like many reading this book, I have made my own mistakes. When I got my Rottie pup at nine weeks old, I used puppy pads, I didn't crate train and I gave her too much freedom too soon. She basically became a puppy landshark, picking up and biting everything in her path. She decimated shoes, books, skirting boards, and then some. And like many others, I initially blamed the dog for her bad behaviour. But quickly I realised that it was me making the mistakes and not her. It was only when I put an actual routine in place that everything started to change. From there I went on to learn all I could about the right and wrong ways to train a dog.

This is my second book. The first was all about how to raise a dog from puppyhood, but this book is going to dig deeper and focus on the issues that we see here at SDT every single day. We will be covering common behavioural problems like leash reactivity, jumping up, excessive barking, reactivity to fireworks, problems at the vets and so much more.

But we won't only be focusing on the dogs; you guys reading are not exempt from my eagle eye either. We will be going through the importance of your state of mind and being consistent in your training, and looking at some crucial techniques to help you relax and embrace your role as a responsible dog owner too. I'm going to share more of my own story with you later as well.

But right now, we are about to go on a journey together, so I hope you are as excited as I am – and if you're not, that's too bad, because you've already paid for the book!

Let's get going . . .

PART I
THE FOUNDATIONS

CHAPTER 1

What to expect

When we start to train a dog at SDT, the very first thing we do is go back to basics. And for us this means checking that there's nothing getting in the way of you and your pet's learning.

We've done the same in this book. You'll see we start in Chapter 2 with checking if your dog is in optimum health, and if a trip to the vet could help with some of the problems you may be experiencing. It's not uncommon for pain or medical issues to be affecting how a dog behaves.

Then in Chapter 3 we move on to explaining SDT's three-point formula for success, covering diet, exercise and teaching the dog an off-switch, which will make sure your dog is at their very best. In Chapter 4, we explore your readiness for training too, because what you do and feel on the other end of the lead is just as important to getting where you want to be. Here we also discuss how to use journalling to track the progress you and your dog make, and at the back of the book you'll find we've included some sample pages so you can take this habit forward.

With this great foundation in place, we'll move on to cover the basics of our training methods in Chapter 5, such as the art of attention and common commands.

From there the book begins to delve much deeper into solving specific behavioural problems you're working with, dedicating chapters to issues such as problems inside the house. In Parts II and III of the book, we cover everything from separation anxiety, multi-dog households, lead walking, socialisation, reactivity and, everyone's favourite, recall! These later chapters will explain what's going wrong and how to fix it.

As you read the book, look out for the QR codes along the way. You can scan these with your smartphone and use the password 'SDTBook' to be taken directly to a relevant training video on our website. This will help you to see the theory we discuss put into practice. You can return to those videos when you want to refresh your learning.

Working through the book in this way will help you reach your training goals in no time.

A QUICK WORD ABOUT RESCUE DOGS

First up though, I want to talk about something that's massively important and something that is dear to my heart. That's right – rescue dogs.

If you don't already have a dog, you might be on the fence about getting an older dog from a rescue centre. You might be thinking about adopting one that could perhaps come with some behavioural baggage but that you feel you can help using the guidelines in this book. Maybe you are an experienced dog owner reading this and are looking to hone your craft and gain more knowledge. If you want to take on a more difficult dog that perhaps has had a traumatic past, keep reading, we've got you.

Let me tell you right now, at the time of writing this book there are approximately 130,000 dogs in UK rescue organisations,[1] and most of them are there through no fault of their own.

Most dogs are surrendered to rescue centres because of human selfishness. Perhaps it was because they didn't do proper research into the breed or because of a dodgy breeder churning out puppies that go on to have problems. Maybe the previous owners couldn't be bothered to put the work in and train the dog when it was a puppy, and now the dog is bigger they can't be arsed and it's a problem. Some dogs are sent to rescue because they aren't fast enough for racing, or because they are surplus to the breeder's requirements. And it's hard to believe but some are just discarded because they get old and grey.

But whatever the reason they end up there, you will find some absolute gems of a dog in these centres. And having worked with thousands of rescues from across the globe and having had my own rescue dogs, I'm telling you now, there is nothing more rewarding than adopting a dog.

Take my little terrier Roxy. She came from a rescue place and had been in a family where there was another dog but no rules. Because she was babied by her owners and not given any direction she began to get into fights with the other dog in the house. When the fighting got serious, Roxy was the one that had to go. Again, it was human incompetence that meant the dog, in this case my Roxy, suffered. Of course, it's not unusual to have

1 https://core.ac.uk/download/pdf/345634869.pdf

problems with multi-dog households and it's something we'll cover in more detail later in the book. These issues can be worked on.

But in the meantime, back to Roxy and why, because of her, I love a rescue.

Poor Roxy was a mess when I met her. Everything scared her: traffic, bikes, loud bangs. And when I say she was terrified, I mean it literally. Things that she was frightened of made her shit herself. I would have to wipe her arse down if a bang went off.

Alongside her fear, she had no idea how to walk on a lead and was reactive to bigger dogs, which was problematic as she came to live here with two bigger dogs that are sadly no longer with us (fuck you, cancer!).

The techniques I used to help this little darling are the techniques I talk about in this book. And those techniques I used on Roxy have given me a small dog that has gone on to help countless other dogs find trust, a dog that loves my children and is always by their side. And this book will help you learn and use these techniques too.

Now Roxy is a confident, entertaining and mischievous pet, and although she's getting on in years, she's the perfect example to me of what a small dog should be. But remember she didn't come like that; it took a lot of hard work, patience and consistency. Regardless of the issues, Roxy shows that you can always help a dog if it's fit and healthy.

So how do you find a rescue that suits you?

Well, first things first, you must be realistic. As rewarding as it is taking on a dog that's a mess, like Roxy was, and turning them around, it takes a lot of skill and time, and isn't for the faint-hearted. If you've never had a dog before, I would instead suggest looking for a more laid-back dog with next-to-no issues. Remember, there are lots of different dogs in rescue so ask questions and meet the dog, or as many dogs as necessary, to find the right fit for both you and your potential pooch. Some dogs in rescue centres may be there as a result of their owner's death or illness or a divorce, and their behaviour will be far less challenging.

The beauty of a rescue is they would have been recently seen by a vet to rule out any serious conditions. They will also have been wormed, treated for fleas and helped with any immediate physical problems, such as skin infections like mange, where necessary. A rescue dog may even have had some formal training from an expert via the organisation looking after it while it waited for a new home. The temperament of a dog up for adoption will also have been fully assessed, and in some cases a history will have been recorded too. This will all help when it comes to finding a perfect match for both you and the dog.

But, of course, a rescue won't suit everyone. You might not be a suitable home for an adopted doggo for several reasons, including if you already own a dog that has issues and needs extra time and help (and if you do, this training guide can help you with that first). Instead, consider regularly donating to your local rescue centre to help them help more dogs, or offer to volunteer your time. You can still help rescue dogs without taking one home.

If you are considering adopting a dog with behavioural issues, and one that you're happy to work on, be honest with yourself because the very worst thing in the world you can do is let that dog down again by returning it. It's about being realistic about your training abilities.

So, let's get cracking...

CHAPTER 2

Health

Something we often find that has been overlooked when a dog displays behavioural problems, and especially reactivity-based issues, is their health. In fact, at SDT one of the first things we ask a client when they get in touch for training and support is 'When was your last vet check?', closely followed by, 'Are there any medical issues we need to be aware of?'

This is so important because dogs can behave uncharacteristically and can become defensive, withdrawn, scared and/or anxious if they're sick or in pain.

A good few years ago I was working with a little Border Terrier who was extremely reactive towards other dogs, but when he was here at SDT we also noticed he was drinking a hell of a lot of water, far more than was normal, and that he was tiring very quickly. The owners themselves were unaware of anything serious going on and had put being tired and drinking more down to him ageing a bit. But, after a vet check, it turned out the dog had diabetes. When his illness was brought under control and managed appropriately, his reactivity all but went away.

This example shows that it's just so important to make sure you keep an eye on the health of your dog and work with a decent vet, a point I'll return to in a moment.

HOW DO YOU KNOW IF THERE'S SOMETHING WRONG WITH YOUR DOG?

Most importantly, you should use your common sense. Remember that you know your dog better than anyone else does. You're the person that spends the most time with your dog and you have an idea of what their base personality is like. If you feel something isn't quite right, or if their behaviour suddenly seems out of the ordinary or different, act on your gut feeling and speak to a vet. That said, there are some common signs of potential health problems you can look for:

Excessive drinking

This can be a sign of poor diet (this is a problem that we will get to in the next chapter) but also a sign of dehydration and/or something more sinister going on.

Not eating

Not to be mistaken for being a fussy eater. If your dog won't take any food when they are usually happy to eat, chances are there could be something wrong.

Restlessness

If your dog seems more restless than normal, it can also be a sign that there is a health issue. Behaviour might include pacing, circling, repeatedly adjusting a sleeping position, or being unable to settle generally.

Reactivity

Sudden unexplained reactivity could be a major indicator that something is wrong. Remember, reactivity can often be a defensive behaviour caused by pain. Signs it's time for a vet visit might include overreacting to situations that your dog would normally take in their stride, by lunging, barking and/or growling.

You can't always see when something is wrong with your dog. While it's easy to spot a problem if the dog is being sick or limping, sometimes you need to use some common sense and understand your dog. A good habit to get into is checking your dog over for any lumps and bumps or abnormalities after each walk, and remember, when in doubt contact a vet!

SO LET'S TALK VETS!

Having a decent vet is worth its weight in gold. But just like how not all dog trainers are created equal, the same goes for vets. I have a vet I use, and he is for the most part the only vet I use, unless it's an out-of-hours emergency. He is straightforward and to the point – there's no beating around the bush and that's something that's so important – plus he knows his stuff. This is a vet that won't guilt you because of your training style, the training equipment you might choose to use, or even the diet your dog is on.

In all my time using this vet, which isn't that often to be fair (the next chapter will explain how you can avoid unnecessary trips to the vet), he has never once tried to force anything on my dogs that they don't need, or onto the clients I send his way. Building a relationship with your vet is also helpful for your dog. The vets can be a scary place for pets; so it's much easier if you can see the same vet every time where possible.

Tips for stress-free vet visits

Now, why is the vets scary, you ask? For a start, your dog is likely going to the vet because there's already something wrong. That means they aren't feeling their best anyway, without anything else coming into play. Then there are previous experiences that your dog associates with the surgery that might be unpleasant. Perhaps they've had jabs, painful exams, or maybe they've even had to stay overnight in the past. Think about it: if you've had root canal work at the dentist, you're hardly going to want to go back and have some more!

The vets can also be overwhelming for a dog, with lots of unfamiliar smells and noise. There are unknown humans and animals, many also giving off fear scents. You might also have limited space to yourself, making your dog feel trapped. And finally, your dog might be able pick up on any anxiety you're feeling about the visit. Yes, there's a lot going on for your dog at the vets.

So, let's go over a few things you can do to help your dog feel as comfortable as possible for those inevitable trips:

- Where possible, request the same vet. Seeing the same face over and over can help your dog relax more.
- Go to the vets on a regular basis, even when your dog doesn't actually need to go. A lot

of vets will allow you to go in, get your dog weighed, and some receptionists will be willing to give your dog a few treats to sweeten the pot. Doing this when your dog isn't sick or in pain will help build a positive association with going to this place where it doesn't always end with the vet pulling and poking around your dog.

- Your mindset matters. Remember, dogs don't understand things the way we do. If you are worrying about your dog, maybe because of its health or because it might not like the vets, your dog won't understand that. What your dog will understand is that when they are stressed and worried, you are stressed and worried. This can often build a negative association to what's in the vicinity, or to the environment itself, either the vet clinic or vet professional.

  As hard as it is, it's important to remain as calm and cool-headed as possible. In Chapter 4 we will dig deep into states of mind and things that can help you relax, which in turn will help your dog to do so too.

- Following the three basic SDT principles will help reduce the likelihood of needing to see the vet. The principles are: 'Diet', 'Exercise' and 'Off Switch', and you need to get all of these right. They are explained in detail in the next chapter. But the healthier your dog is in body and mind, the less likely they are going to need to go to the vets for treatment.

- Crate train your dog. A lot of the time, if a dog needs to have an operation it will go into a crate/kennel pre- and post-op, and you may even be advised to put your dog on crate rest after an operation too. So, it follows that we don't want the first experience of being in a crate to be at the vets or after an operation. That can be more stressful for the dog and lead to more problems with negative associations. Making sure your dog is comfortable in a crate will help with so many problems, but will also help massively with vet issues and with recovery. Full crate-training advice can be found on p.60.
- Some dogs may require a muzzle at the vets because, as mentioned before, when a dog is in pain they can behave uncharacteristically. Again, you don't want to wait until a time of stress/pain to introduce the muzzle, which can be stressful itself, so make sure your dog is properly muzzle conditioned beforehand. If the only time the muzzle is on is at the vets, in your dog's mind the vets is a bad place where bad things happen. So, you need to make sure muzzle training is a part of your regular training – and make it fun.

MUZZLE TRAINING

All dogs should be able to be muzzled. No ifs, not buts, no maybes. Every fucking dog on the planet should be trained to wear a muzzle. Now that doesn't mean your dog should have to wear it all the time, but knowing your dog is comfortable in a muzzle will give you peace of mind and help you both be prepared for when it is necessary. I've never had to regularly muzzle any of my dogs, past or present, but I know if I did have to, they could wear one, and with no problems at all. And this is because I have trained them to accept a muzzle, whether they need it or not.

Muzzles should always be worn in public if your dog has made attempts to bite or will bite given the chance. This should be something you take very seriously. Remember, if your dog bites someone, that could be game over for your dog. A muzzle is literally the difference between a bite happening or not. Which means it could also be the difference between your dog being potentially seized and put to sleep, or not.

Of course, a muzzle alone won't fix a behaviour problem; you can't slap a muzzle on and think your work is done. The law requires that your dog must always be under control. And if your dog is lunging and trying to get to someone or something, or running riot, that means it's not under control, muzzle or not. So, a muzzle should be used to keep your dog, and those around it, safe while you are training your dog to be fully under control.

Reactivity is not the only reason to muzzle a dog. A muzzle might also be necessary if your dog is a scavenger. Picking up discarded or poisonous food or other rubbish can put your dog's health at risk. A muzzle will also protect wild animals if your dog has a high prey drive and equally fast legs.

In fact, we should embrace muzzles and their use a lot more – and stop assuming that all dogs in muzzles are bad or have bad owners. On the contrary, owners who muzzle their dogs, who are going through training and putting the time and effort into helping their dog and keeping others safe, are truly the good owners.

Choosing a muzzle

There are really only two main types of muzzles, one of which we recommend for general use. You must make sure the style you choose is right for your dog, particularly if your pet has a short, long, wide, or narrow snout. It goes without saying (I hope) that your dog must be able to breathe while wearing its muzzle. If the muzzle is going to stay on for a little while, they must be able to pant and drink, and take a treat. When you get the right style and fit of muzzle for your dog, you can relax knowing it's safe and effective.

Basket/Baskerville muzzles

These look exactly like they sound, like a basket strapped to your dog's nose and mouth. They can be made of leather, wire, plastic or even rubber, and can be bought off the shelf or customised to fit your dog's face shape. Even flat-faced dogs like pugs can wear muzzles if they fit properly. And while basket muzzles can look intimidating to us humans, this type of muzzle is very comfortable for your dog, as its mouth isn't being held closed and they can pant, drink and eat.

SDT sells the Baskerville muzzle, which allows dogs to pant and drink. This design means it's suitable for daily walks and longer time periods. We sell two types of Baskerville muzzles, which allows dogs to pant and drink. They are suitable for daily walks and longer time periods. One of the muzzles is specially designed and comes with an additional removable guard insert to prevent scavenging; when the guard is removed you can train and treat reward your dog. Baskerville muzzles are made of strong plastic and are safe for reactive dogs and bite prevention. They also come in a range of sizes and with a secure and easy-to-use neck strap clip attachment. It is comfortable for your dog because of the padded nose.

Soft muzzles

Usually made from a fabric such as nylon, mesh, or sometimes leather, soft muzzles are designed to wrap around your dog's mouth and hold it tightly closed. This kind of muzzle can only be used for a very short period and never in hot weather. This is because soft muzzles prevent your dog from barking, drinking, eating and, most importantly, panting, which is the only way it has of cooling down (panting is like sweating for us), making them potentially dangerous if left on. The design also means it's very hard to use treats as a reward or distraction from something unpleasant, even when you're training your dog to get used to this type of muzzle. Soft muzzles are primarily designed for vet visits only, so that a dog that is a bite risk can be examined safely.

Fit your muzzle properly

Getting the right fit is key to using a muzzle correctly, so you'll need to measure your dog's nose to find the right size. If a muzzle is too big, your dog will be able to remove it or might get it stuck somewhere, but if a muzzle is too tight it could cause uncomfortable rubbing. And an incorrectly fitted muzzle can also stop your dog being able to breathe, pant or drink. You should be able to fit one finger between your dog and the strap at the back of the dog's head.

To help you get the right fit, try on various sizes and ask an expert (like your dog trainer) for their opinion.

When should you not use a muzzle?

Muzzles are designed for one thing and one thing only: to stop dog bites. They are a training tool.

You should not be using a muzzle to force your dog's mouth shut instead of actually working on a behavioural problem such as barking or chewing.

Using a muzzle in the wrong way can also cause more problems. Say your dog finds mixing with other dogs difficult and tries to lunge at and bite them. Putting a muzzle on your dog while forcing them into situations they find difficult will stop your dog from harming other dogs yes, but it will not stop it from reacting. The underlying problem is still there; your dog will continue forming negative associations with that scenario and now your dog will also begin to associate wearing the muzzle with that stressful situation. This means your dog could get worked up as soon as it sees the muzzle, knowing that something it finds difficult is about to happen.

Muzzles should not be used for punishment either. Instead of fixing an underlying behaviour problem, if you use a muzzle to punish your dog, it will simply attach negative associations to the muzzle. And now if you need to muzzle your dog in an emergency, your dog will be even more scared.

Getting your dog used to the muzzle

So, we've established there are plenty of reasons why muzzle training your dog is a good thing. Now you need to know how to do it!

The first time you put a muzzle on your dog should not be the first time you *need* to put one on. If your dog's first introduction to wearing a muzzle comes at a time when they are hurt or scared, then not only will it be much more difficult to get the muzzle on, the chances of getting a muzzle easily on your dog again in the future are slim.

To avoid any negative associations with the muzzle you should introduce your dog to one long before you need it, and in a step-by-step and non-stressful way. All dogs can be trained to accept a muzzle if they are introduced to it properly, typically by rewarding the dog in stages along the way. Make sure your dog is 100 per cent okay with each step before moving to the next.

Here's what to do:

- **Step 1** Show your dog the muzzle and let him sniff it. Give your dog a treat/praise. Repeat this a few times.
- **Step 2** Touch your dog's nose with the muzzle. Then treat/praise. Repeat this step until your dog shows he is happy to see the muzzle.
- **Step 3** Hold the muzzle with one hand and a treat with the other hand, holding the treat so that your dog needs to put his nose inside the muzzle to get it. Again, repeat this step until your dog is happy doing this.
- **Step 4** Now move on to gently slipping the muzzle onto your dog's nose, giving him a treat when you do so. Remove the muzzle immediately. Repeat this until you're sure your dog is happy.
- **Step 5** Put the muzzle on your dog and this time fasten the buckle. Give your dog a treat and remove the muzzle immediately. Do this a few times and check your dog is still happy.
- **Step 6** Put the muzzle on your dog, fasten it and count slowly to five. Give your dog a treat and remove the muzzle. Gradually increase the time the muzzle is on your dog, treating your dog in the process.

How To Train Your Dog

'Password: SDTBook'

TAKEAWAYS

- Health is often overlooked when a dog displays behavioural problems
- You know your dog better than anyone else; if you think there's something wrong, talk to a vet
- Excessive drinking, not eating, restlessness and reactivity can all be signs of a health problem
- Finding a vet you trust and building a relationship with them is helpful for your dog
- Vet visits can be overwhelming for a dog; make it less stressful by conditioning your pet to feel comfortable with regular trips there just for a fuss and treat

- Every dog needs to be muzzle trained in case of emergency; the best time to do this is well before you need to
- Muzzle train your dog slowly using our 6-step process

CHAPTER 3

The SDT three-point formula

So now we have covered the importance of making sure your dog is medically fit, how do we make sure your dog is also physically and mentally ready to learn? I'm about to go over the three-point formula that I swear by. And it's not just a formula that works for your dog; it also offers massive health benefits to us humans too.

I've spent the last ten years working on these key pillars of dog training, and if you commit to them and get it right, you can help any dog, regardless of the issues you're experiencing. It won't cure all behaviour problems, but it will help with virtually any issue you have with your dog.

POINT 1 – DIET

That's right, people: diet. What we put into our bodies matters. Diet plays a massive part in our health. Put simply, if you eat shit, you feel like shit. A poor diet can affect our energy levels, our skin, our mood and our behaviour. It can affect our bodies both inside and out, for better or for worse. It's the same for a dog.

Now most people, when they think of a dog diet, might think of the mainstream dog food brands they are used to seeing on TV or in the supermarkets. But a lot of the time these mainstream brands you are so familiar with are some of the worst foods on the market; it's just that they have huge advertising budgets.

So how do you know what's a good food and what's not?

It's simple. When you look at dog food, you want to check the ingredients, and the first ingredient *must* be a high percentage of meat, somewhere in the region of 25 per cent if you're looking at bagged food. If it says meat derivatives or – worse – cereal, you are giving your dog garbage in a sack. You also want to avoid foods with lots of additives and preservatives.

If you were to give your child Skittles for breakfast, lunch and dinner every day, they would be bouncing off the walls. They would struggle to concentrate and very quickly you would see some major health problems. Using some of these mainstream dog food brands is like giving your dog Skittles every single day. It's not hard to find a connection between diet and hyperactive behaviours in dogs. I see dogs riddled with allergies, poor skin, foul-smelling breath, poor teeth and gums, and poor bowel movements, and often when we dig deeper we see that the diet plays a massive part in these problems.

What you feed your dog matters. A decent diet can reduce trips to the vets, can make your dog's life better, and can even help with training.

Raw feeding

So, what do we recommend here at SDT? Well, I've been feeding my dogs raw food longer than I can remember. It's a species-appropriate diet; it's everything a dog needs.

A proper raw-food diet has proper fresh meat in it. My late Rottweiler used to suffer terribly with ear infections, while my late Staffie used to suffer badly with her anal glands. Switching to raw solved both these issues in my own dogs.

Sammie's blocked anal glands used to make her grumpy with other dogs; she would behave defensively (not aggressively) if they went near her back end, which is a natural area for a dog to sniff. We would take her to the vets, they would sort her anal glands and she would be fine again. But it was a never-ending cycle. Good for a while then back at square one. When I looked into diet, I was shocked to find it could be a reason for anal gland problems, so I switched the diet and BOOM! Problem solved. She never had any issues again in that department.

So now you see how important diet is when it comes to dogs in terms of health *and* behaviour.

Now, I get raw food might not be for everyone; some people don't like to handle raw meat, some people don't have the freezer space, and some people see the importance of hand feeding – a topic we will come to later in this book. But raw feeding and hand feeding raw food can be a bit of a bollock ache.

So, if raw isn't for you, then what?

Well, we sell raw food for dogs, but we also sell cold press raw food, which has all the benefits of raw food but without the need for a freezer. It feels more like kibble (dry food) in texture and is much easier to store. Both cold press and raw can be purchased through our website, but we are not the only suppliers; lots of companies sell it.

Even if we haven't convinced you to try raw or cold press, then at the very least make sure the food you are feeding is premium food. Make sure the first ingredient is a high percentage of meat and make sure there are not lots of unnecessary ingredients in it.

How To Train Your Dog

'Password: SDTBook'

Weight issues

So many dogs now are overweight. But overfeeding your dog isn't spoiling them, it's killing them with kindness. A fat dog has a shorter life expectancy. A fat dog is more prone to health problems, such as diabetes and cancers to name just two, and is more likely to have joint problems, which can cause pain and lead to behaviour problems.

Overweight dogs get hotter quicker, tire quicker, get irritable quicker, and that comes from all the extra weight on their joints and vital organs. Overfeeding your dog, giving them human food, or giving them food that isn't good for them is a big problem. A dog should be able to run and function; they should not be blowing steam just for walking down the road or jumping on the sofa.

Of course, some people feed their dogs the appropriate amount, yet their dogs are still fat. And how does this happen? Well, it's primarily down to...exercise!

POINT 2 – EXERCISE

Again, just like humans, exercise, or rather lack of it, can cause many problems for dogs and not just the obvious one of obesity.

Imagine it from the dog's perspective. Nearly all dogs were originally bred to work and developed with specific skill sets to be good at certain tasks. Now imagine all that greatness that dogs were bred for not being used either at work or play. How frustrating is that? And where will that energy end up going instead? Perhaps it won't surprise you to learn that lack of exercise in dogs can cause behaviour problems such as anxiety, excessive barking, hyperactivity and destructiveness, to name just a few.

And by exercise we don't just mean going to the dog park, throwing a ball over and over again or letting your dog play with other dogs running free every day. In fact, all this sort of exercise is doing is building an adrenaline junkie that can go and go for days. And worse still, if your dog is playing with other dogs every day outside the house, guess what? In comparison to his friends at the dog park, you suck! Those other dogs will become way more important to your pet than you ever will. And that's a nightmare for bonding and training.

So how do we get it right? What is proper exercise for dogs? At SDT, we believe proper exercise consists of three things: mental stimulation, breed fulfilment and physical enrichment.

Mental stimulation

What do we mean by mental stimulation? This is when your dog is thinking, when your dog is using its brain, when its nose is working and all those fantastic natural instincts kick in.

How can you do this? Here are some ideas...

Did you know that a good structured 60-minute sniffing walk somewhere new can be way more tiring for your dog than the same amount of time spent playing with other dogs? Try a new place at a slow pace and see how much more satisfied your dog is at the end of the walk.

Add in some basic obedience skills on every walk, ideally at random times so your dog must pay attention and think. This will get that dog brain engaged and reinforce your training, helping your results.

Mental stimulation is way more tiring for your dog than you might think. And if we combine it with physical exercise too, well, we are really getting somewhere.

Breed fulfilment

Mental stimulation can be further expanded from the more general examples given above to also include some breed fulfilment specific to the type of dog you have. Think about giving your dog a job, ideally something they were designed to do many moons ago, or something very similar.

For instance, adding searching games into your walks for a spaniel will be awesome, because they are bred to hunt, flushing out game. Adding a flirt pole, which is essentially a stick with an enticing 'lure' attached to it, into your training will be great for those breeds with a strong prey drive, like sight hounds, who love to chase.

Carrying something can be great for those dogs who are designed to pull, like sledging and herding breeds. Typically, this would be a backpack, a type of weighted harness that the dog wears where you can add weight. A typical healthy dog will carry 5 to 10 per cent of their body weight. Getting your dog to carry a backpack also gives him the sense of carrying something, which can slow a dog down and help them focus. Backpacks are suitable for dogs that have no joint or health problems and are fully grown. If in any doubt about your own dog's suitability to a backpack, consult a vet.

But even if you can't do what the dog was designed to do, because they are too young, too old, have a health limitation, or it's just not practical, giving your dog tasks, even basic obedience, is asking them to do something and work for something.

Adding specific breed fulfilment tasks, or at the very least giving your dog a job, can prevent these traits coming out in other areas when it's less desirable. One of the most common issues I see with herding breeds is traffic reactivity; 99 per cent of the time, these dogs are lacking breed fulfilment and proper exercise.

Physical enrichment

Physical exercise is great for everybody, and your dog is no exception. For a dog, exercise keeps him fit and it keeps him healthy, BUT again, physical exercise doesn't always mean just run, run and run some more. You could take a nice long sniff walk instead, and that's physically and mentally enriching at the same time.

Running is good for some dogs. Some dogs like to chase. Some dogs love a game of fetch, so this is also fine, but make the dog work for the ball. Make them do two or three different commands before giving them the ball. This will be way more powerful and enriching for your dog and for his training.

The life expectancy of dogs seems to be getting shorter, behaviour problems seem to be getting worse and, in my opinion, so much of this is down to lack of exercise. Most people don't give their dogs nearly enough physical exercise. It's the same with a lot of people: we are stuck indoors glued to phones and other screens, stuffing our faces with junk.

Most healthy dogs need about two hours minimum of exercise a day, some types and breeds more, some less. If you have a working breed like a Border Collie, which was designed to work on a farm all day long, and you just take it for 45–60 minutes' exercise at the same park every day, don't be surprised if that dog starts going mental and develops behaviour issues. It's common sense that you're not providing enough mental and physical stimulation for this type of dog.

Remember, guys, dogs were bred to do so much more than go to the bloody dog park and play with other dogs. And this is why so many behaviour issues occur in our dogs. Dog parks should be renamed disease-riddled fight clubs, or where you go for your obedience to die! So many accidents happen in places like this. Often you will have dogs with no recall running over, their owners in the distance shouting 'it's okay, he's friendly!' because they have no control over their dog. Ask yourself if this is the type of dog you want in your dog's life. There is nothing normal about a bunch of strange dogs from different households all congregating in one place and being expected to all get along with each other.

So many fights happen in dog parks because the dogs are out of control for the most part. There are dogs that are being bullies, and dogs being bullied. It's just not a place where anything magical happens. For our training to be effective, we want to be the centre of our dog's universe, and we don't want other dogs to take up that position. More on this later.

Another mistake when it comes to exercise is thinking that our dogs need more of the same to tire them out because we've in fact created an adrenaline junkie that can't calm down. If you are going out with your dog for one to two hours, and you've done lots of mental and physical enrichment, but when you come home your dog still wants to play, chances are this is because he doesn't know how to switch off. You don't need to take your dog out for three, four or five walks a day to wear them out. They need just one or two good walks, and then to be taught about the off switch.

POINT 3 – THE OFF SWITCH

The final part to my three-point formula is switching off, and it's vital. It should be universal for all dogs to master at the beginning of training. They need to learn that after the adrenaline of a walk or other forms of mental and physical stimulation, it's time for rest and to switch off.

Dogs that don't know how to settle can become adrenaline junkies, which is never a good thing. A lot of anxiety-based and/or destructive behaviours can be caused by a dog's inability to decompress. When you teach a dog to switch off, you're teaching a life skill that will enable you to go on to enjoy lots of activities together, such as a long walk followed by a trip to a pub or a restaurant, where the dog can be put into a 'Down, Stay' while you and your family/friends enjoy your drink or meal. A dog that knows how to settle is a happy dog.

But some dogs really do struggle more than others to switch off. Some dogs just don't know how to, and this is especially true for breeds like spaniels, German Shepherds, Pointers, etc. If your dog is like this, he needs to be taught how to switch off. How do we achieve this? We crate train. If you'd like to learn the right way to crate train, turn to Chapter 5 where we discuss all our basic training (p.60).

And what starts with crate training leads to what we at SDT call the 'Art of Doing Nothing'. Whenever your dog needs to chill out – at the vets, at the train station, in a shop or a pub, while you stop and chat to a friend, or even at home when nothing is going on, or when lots is going on but you don't want them going crazy – they will be practising the Art of Doing Nothing. And once it's perfected, you'll move on from using a crate for this. Your dog will progress to doing nothing on his bed, or maybe the sofa, or, if you're out and about, on a carpet or floor or pavement.

CONCLUSION

Guys, if you want to have a happy, healthy, contented dog, make sure you really stick to these three things from the SDT formula. I can tell you, if your dog has behaviour problems this will help massively. A tired dog that's fed properly and knows how to switch off isn't getting up to no good. Remember that. I'm also a big believer in this for humans as well. Having a dog can do wonders for you physically and mentally. Getting out in the fresh air, exercising, watching what you eat and making sure you take time to decompress will have an overwhelming impact on you.

TAKEAWAYS

- SDT has developed a three-point formula for a happy dog. Get diet, exercise and an off switch right, and you're going to be looking at a happy dog and a happy owner
- If you eat shit, you feel like shit, and it's the same for your dog – check the dog food you use is a quality one
- Always check the meat content on dog food, and avoid additives and preservatives
- We recommend raw feeding – or cold pressed raw food
- Lack of exercise can cause many problems for dogs, including obesity. It can cause behaviour problems such as anxiety, excessive barking, hyperactivity and destructiveness
- Exercise should be both mental and physical, and take into account breed fulfilment
- It's vital to teach your dog about switching off. The best way to teach a dog to switch off is by crate training
- The SDT formula will work for you AND your dog!

CHAPTER 4

State of mind

As I begin this chapter, I sit here and think how important this message is. You see today wasn't a good day for me; it was actually the day we did the photoshoot for the front cover of this book, and it didn't go exactly to plan; there were some hiccups.

The lovely dog you see on the front cover is Roxy. She can do just about anything: her focus is great, recall is great, stays are on point, lead walking excellent – you name it, she can do it. But she doesn't like being picked up for longer periods of time. In fact she hates it and it's something we have never worked on really, because it's not something that's overly important in everyday life. Until you come to doing a photoshoot, and things get difficult! Of course, being the perfectionist I am, it took a while to get some decent photos because of this issue, but these things happen, I guess.

So, take from this that even dog trainers' dogs are not perfect and have their flaws; even dog trainers can have bad days; and, yes, you will have bad days along your journey too.

Those bad days could be with your training or even in your life, but let me tell you: IT'S OKAY! It's okay to not be perfect all the time. It's okay to make mistakes.

It's okay to not be in the best state of mind. It's okay, and don't ever let anyone tell you otherwise.

But I can't tell you how important being in the right state of mind is when we are working with dogs. There is no faking it. They will see right through you. If you are nervous, they know it; anxious, they know it; angry, they know it. In fact, dogs will even mirror their owners so it's not uncommon for a nervous dog to have a nervous owner or confident owners to have confident dogs. But sometimes we can't help our state of mind. Sometimes we have baggage so deep, the demons that plague us can go on to affect our dogs.

MY STORY

That was me. In fact, as I try to put all this into words that will help you guys, I'm coming up on eighteen months sober. I'm about to share something that only those who are closest to me know about.

I've struggled my whole life with anxiety, insecurities and addiction.

For me, it stems from my childhood and teenage years. I was exposed to stuff at a young age that stuck with me, and my social circle and the prominent male figures in my life were all about 'Boys don't cry, boys don't moan, shove it down, man up and get on with it.' That's a bad path. It turns out the medicine I found to help me was drugs and alcohol. If I was nervous, I would drink. If I was anxious, I would drink. If I was angry, I would drink. It was a coping mechanism.

This pattern carried on into adulthood. I didn't even realise I had an issue at the time, I was very much in denial, but that soon changed as the SDT business grew. The more followers we got, the more we were in the public eye; the more the company grew, the more pressure I felt. That pressure led to anxiety. Completely understandable, right? But, of course, to make it okay, I would just get off my face. And it nearly cost me everything. I was a ghost in my own company; I wasn't doing what I needed to do. Even worse, I wasn't being a good father or husband. I was dragging down those who cared so much for me, and I nearly lost it all.

As they say, admitting you have a problem is the first step.

I had to do something, and so I went to Narcotics Anonymous. This is where I realised that drugs and alcohol were a problem for me, but they were really the fallout from much bigger problems. I started talking to people in similar situations to myself, sharing stories about my day. I was shocked to see how many successful people were there, businesspeople, CEOs, etc., and this also helped because I no longer felt alone. I didn't stay there for long because I kept getting recognised by people and that made me more anxious, so I went private, but the thing that helped me was talking.

Talking to a stranger, talking about what was on my mind, talking about my feelings for the first time, allowing myself to get emotional and dig deep into self-awareness. Learning how my actions affected others. In the past, the one thing I never did was talk, and that leads to bottling everything up and eventually exploding.

And let me tell you, if you are not looking after yourself, you can't help anyone. This is also why I'm a big advocate of everything I explained in Chapter 3. Eating right is game-changing. Exercising is game-changing. And taking some time for yourself to decompress is essential. Going to the gym has been a game-changer for me. It's not just about getting healthy physically but also mentally. Exercise makes you feel better about yourself, which in turn affects other areas of your life.

In the beginning challenge yourself just to turn up and commit, and then it gets fun. Switch off, take time for yourself – it's so important. You could be setting aside time to watch a film, read a book, go to a spa – anything that's just for you! Like I said, game-changer.

And don't forget the importance of your diet. Remember we discussed in the last chapter that if your dog eats shit food, they will feel like shit? Well, it's the same for you too. Eating the right foods will make you feel better inside and out and have a massive impact on your mental and physical well-being.

My top piece of advice is, don't bottle things up. Get it out there, even if it's on paper. It helps massively.

WRITE IT DOWN

Journalling is something I learned about when I was starting on the road to recovery. Writing about your day, the good, the bad and the ugly, putting it all down on paper, is a massive help. I write about what I am thankful for, what really matters, the important stuff, as well as making lists on everything from things you're grateful for and that went well that day, to those things that are stressing you out and causing frustration. This creates self-awareness; you start to see patterns in your behaviour and things you can work on. It's an act of mindfulness, and just getting your feelings out onto paper (or your screen) helps you reflect and deal with them. And you can apply this to dog training. When you are out with your dog or training, write down things like the time of day, your mood, where you went, how long for and a brief summary of the walk. An example:

> *3 pm: I'm feeling okay. Reggie was really disconnected and unfocused, there were lots of children and foot traffic around, it was stressful. The walk was around 60 minutes.*

Journalling didn't seem that important to me at first, but, I tell you, it's huge, it's a game-changer. After a week you will see patterns in what you've written and be able to work on and change things for the better. At the back of the book, we've provided some sample pages to help you get journalling successfully.

BREATHE

Another technique that's really beneficial is deep breathing when you are out and about, especially if you are feeling stressed, nervous or worried about the situation. Slow down, take deep breaths and count to ten slowly in your head or out loud. It will calm you down, slow down your heart rate and have a huge impact on your dog as well as yourself.

FOCUS ON THE POSITIVES

Remember, there are 24 hours in a day, and if your dog misbehaves for 20 minutes, there were 23 hours and 40 minutes that he was good. There are seven days in a week; if you have six good walks but one bad, don't let that undo the feel-good from the hard work you've put in. Don't let the little bit of bad ruin everything else. Focus on the positives.

As humans we are crap at celebrating the successes but excellent at focusing on the negatives, but how you look at things has a massive impact. If you are feeling stressed, do something easy with your dog like a slow sniff walk, or a game of fetch in a quiet location. If you are in good stead, push yourself. Remember, you are not alone, there is help out there – help in this book, help in person, for your dog and for you. Don't sit and suffer alone.

I'm always here for you, and don't ever let anyone tell you you are not good enough or you can't do it, because you fucking can!

I believe in you.

TAKEAWAYS

- Even dog trainers have bad days, and as you train your dog you will likely have bad days too
- It's okay to not be perfect all the time
- Being in the right state of mind when we are working with dogs is important
- Look after your physical and mental health, just as you would for your dog
- Journalling your day creates self-awareness and can help you see patterns of behaviour in you and your dog
- Don't let the little mistakes in training ruin everything; focus on the positive
- If you're struggling, seek help
- Turn to the back of the book for some sample journalling pages

CHAPTER 5

The basics

Now that we have discussed the three core principles to having a happy dog and the importance of state of mind, it's time to work on your basic commands. These are things that every dog should be taught, and once you've mastered them, everything else will be so much easier. So, let's dig right in.

THE ART OF ATTENTION

This is one of the foundations that everything else is built upon. Once you have your dog's attention, the sky is the limit. But so many people struggle with this because their dog's attention is on everything but them.

The art of attention is easy to master though, and it's one of the simplest things you can teach. It works like this: before your dog gets *anything* fun or exciting, you simply wait for eye contact and then give them what they want.

Before feeding them, before leaving the house for a walk, before going in and out of the garden, before being released from a sit-stay or down-stay, before throwing a ball, *wait for eye contact.* This teaches your dog that you are the key to all things fun and exciting, and that makes you the centre of their universe.

You must make the art of attention a lifestyle. Something that becomes second nature to your dog. You don't use a voice command for eye contact in the beginning, no command is needed for this; just your marker word – which we explain below – once eye contact is made.

The reason for this is simple. A lot of dogs see eye contact as a stressful thing, so saying 'watch me' and forcing your dog to make eye contact can be difficult. So simply waiting for the dog to offer eye contact makes it a much more rewarding and stress-free experience.

Eventually, when it's second nature, you can begin to pair a command to it if you wish.

MARKERS AND REINFORCEMENT

Markers are key words that indicate a dog has done what you've asked or is doing what you've asked, and a reward is to follow. They are essential.

You can use verbal markers or clicker markers, but they are not to be mistaken for commands. Commands are something you ask the dog to do: for example, 'Sit', 'Down', 'Come' or 'Heel'. Markers are to mark the behaviour you like and let them know a reward is coming.

The markers we use are as follows:

The 'Yes' marker

We use this to signify the dog has done what we have asked them to do and to come to us to get a reward. The easiest way to teach this is to put the dog in a sit, wait for eye contact (remember, the art of attention is vital), say

'Yes' and step back. This will bring the dog towards you, and you can then give them the reward. Using the 'Yes' marker means the command has been completed and is over.

'Yes' is one of the most powerful words you can drum into your dog. It builds motivation like no other.

The 'Good' marker

We use this marker as a duration marker or a continuous marker. If you want your dog to keep doing something and want to let them know you are happy with it, the marker 'Good' is useful. 'Good' gives the dog an incentive to keep doing that command you've asked.

An example would be when your dog is in a down, you say 'Good' and give your dog a treat (sometimes you may have to remind the dog to stay in that down in the beginning, but they will soon learn 'Good' means a reward is coming to them, so they'll stay right there doing what they're doing). Using the 'Good' marker means the command is ongoing.

The 'Break' marker

'Break' is the final marker we use. This is a marker that shows the exercise is over. Like 'Free dog' if you will. The reward is the dog is free from whatever you were doing.

Alternatively, the reward comes from the environment. You could use 'Break', for example, in a situation where letting the dog off the lead is the reward. You could ask the dog to sit, wait for eye contact and then say 'Break'. The dog is now free to enjoy some off-lead time. That's the reward.

The easiest way to remember these are:

- 'Yes' means come to me for a reward.
- 'Good' means keep doing it, I'm coming to you to give you a reward.
- 'Break' means free dog.

Clicker training

Using a clicker as a marker to help with your training can also be a great option, particularly if you've got some more serious behaviours you want to work on such as reactivity. But before you use a clicker your dog has to understand what the clicker means, so the very first thing you need to do is build that positive association to the sound of the clicker. It's very simple: to let the dog know the clicker is a good thing, just practise clicking and rewarding several times over (click click, reward, click click, reward). The reason we often go 'click click' or double-tap on the clicker is because the sound is more distinctive.

Your aim is to get your dog's attention on you, so you want your dog to look at you as soon as it hears the click. Once this is happening, you're ready to go.

The clicker relies on your being able to give your dog a treat, so if your dog is not food motivated, you may need to stop feeding all food from the bowl, and instead use the daily food allowance as rewards instead of offering any extras. This should help bring out your dog's food drive.

REINFORCEMENT AND REINFORCEMENT

That's not a typo guys, I want to talk about the two meanings of reinforcement. We reinforce by using conditioning in the form of rewards, and we also reinforce the commands we use.

The first meaning covers the rewards for the dog that you immediately deliver after using markers. They are the rewards that work as the 'reinforcement incentives' for the dog to do as asked. Payment, if you will, for jobs done well.

But we are also going to talk about your reinforcement of the commands that are given, because this is where so many people fail in training. You must be consistent with your commands and what you expect when you give them. Each time you use a command you must look for the same result, irrespective of where you are – at home or away from the house – and if you are alone or around other dogs.

But let's start with the fun. It's always best to add some positive reinforcement into your training when teaching your dog something new, or when your dog is doing something you like, even if you haven't asked for it.

What you use for reinforcement will differ from dog to dog. For me I'm a big advocate for hand feeding so I use a lot of food in my training, and I'm also an advocate for play, so I use a lot of toys in my training too.

But it's important to listen to your dog and to what it's trying to tell you, especially when you are out and about. Some dogs are avid sniffers, some dogs like to run, some dogs like to play rough, and some dogs like to mooch around. When you spot what it is that your dog most likes to do, try to incorporate it as a reward after you've asked for something.

For example, if you are out working on lead walking, you might choose to let your dog sniff and explore as a reward, as opposed to using food at that moment. If your dog likes to run, you might want to incorporate a flirt pole into your training so the dog can chase something as reinforcement after some obedience.

Finding the right reinforcement for the moment can be a real game-changer.

Food rewards we recommend:

Typically, when training dogs, we recommend hand feeding. What this means is, instead of feeding your dog from a bowl, you take your dog's daily food allowance and you stick that in a treat pouch, and this is what you use for all of your food reinforcement. The beauty of this is every time the dog does something you ask or something you like, you're always in a position to reward them.

If you're not hand feeding, because I understand that's not for everyone, then here are some of the treats that we do recommend at a very high value that dogs seem to love: the SDT cold press (this is great for training rewards, even the fussiest dogs seem to like this!), we also have things like tripe sticks, dehydrated meats or JR Pure Pate. In my experience, these all seem to be very high value treats for the dogs that we've been working with.

Toys we recommend for reinforcement:

- Chuckit balls (not tennis balls)

Tennis balls are bad for your dog's teeth, as the material they are made of acts like sandpaper on those pearly whites. A Chuckit ball is the same size as a tennis ball but much kinder to your dog's canines. Remember to warm up to using a ball, rather than just throwing it over and over again. It's a good opportunity to ask the dog to do something before the ball is thrown, even a basic 'Sit'.

◆ Tug toys

Tug toys are great for dogs like Staffies and bulldogs who like to wrestle and play rough, but many other breeds, including German Shepherds and Collies, also love a good tug game. Tug doesn't make your dog aggressive; it's actually a great close-contact bonding game you can play with your dog to expend energy and use for reinforcement during obedience training. A tug toy can be used to help teach commands such as 'Fetch' and 'Leave it'. The only dogs I wouldn't be using this type of toy with would be dogs who guard toys from humans. More on that in later chapters.

A rope or bite wedge toy is great (a bite wedge is an ergonomically shaped toy designed to fit a dog's mouth). This should be something the dog can grab hold of and use to play with you, rather than play with by itself. And I'll explain why that's important in a moment.

◆ Flirt pole

A flirt pole basically looks like a giant cat toy.

It's a pole and at one end there's some sort of a rope with a toy attached to that. Flirt poles provide an outlet for chasing. A lot of dogs love to chase things but can't be allowed to do so for many reasons, so this is a great addition to your training that fulfils that need in an appropriate way. The flirt pole is great for dogs with high prey drives, dogs who love to run and chase, and it can be really tiring. Combine it with obedience training and you're onto a winner.

A word of warning with a flirt pole and young puppies, however. Remember, a young dog is still growing, and its joints are vulnerable. Exercise caution when you use a flirt pole with a dog that is still growing so you don't overwork it.

Too many toys

And that's it when it comes to toys for reinforcement, just the three options. You see, your dog doesn't need a whole box full. Too many toys can create a fussy, spoilt dog who lacks toy drive and worse. If they have free access to them, they can even begin to guard them from other animals and humans too.

Now some people might think this is harsh, but if you are exercising your dog properly, if you are following Chapter 3 to a tee, your dog won't need toys to keep it occupied in the house as it will be sleeping and relaxing.

Think of it this way: if your dog can go and get a toy out of its toy box and play with it by itself, why does it need you? With easy access to a whole range of toys, the dog can play with its toys in the house whenever it wants, so why would it want that as a reward at another time, such as when it's around dogs or people or other exciting and novel distractions in the real world?

I like to play with my dogs and their toys outside the house, starting the exercise and finishing it. I like to keep it short and sweet in the beginning and leave the dog wanting more. The aim is for the dog to consider playing with me as a reward.

If you need something to keep your dog occupied from time to time, then we recommend interactive toys such as Kongs that can be stuffed with ingredients such as kibble, and brain puzzles, which will encourage your dog to work to get treats or rewards. Again, these come out when you need them, and the dog doesn't have free access to them.

Another thing to bear in mind is that if you have one dog, free access to toys might not be a problem, but it could become problematic when you add a second dog into the mix. You might be thinking of getting another dog later, or you might have guest dogs stay from time to time. Either way, toys could cause friction between two dogs.

Whether it's hand feeding or whether it's treats, toys or whatever you use to reinforce training, when you're using these things as a reward for a job well done, make sure you pay well in the beginning until you've absolutely nailed it. Bear in mind, when adolescence kicks in, your dog can regress too, so you need to always remind your dog that doing as you ask pays, and pays well!

USING COMMANDS EFFECTIVELY

Now let's talk about the reinforcement of the commands you give. This is so simple yet so many people don't realise they are not letting the dog know what is expected of it.

If you ask a dog to sit, sit should mean sit – not sit for a second and then get back up. The dog should sit until you release them from the sit or give them further instructions. Same as if you send them to their bed, place them in a down or recall them. (Do remember, however, that there are some dog breeds that are physiologically less able to sit for long periods of time, and 'Down' may be more comfortable for them.)

The mistake people make is that when it's just them and the dog, they let them get away with not following the instruction until release. But when there's a major distraction, such as another dog in the local park, they do expect the dog to behave. This makes life so much harder. And it makes a dog's life so much harder too. If your dog has learnt that he doesn't have to hold positions until he is released, when there is a major distraction the dog follows the same pattern, and doesn't wait for the 'free dog' marker before heading off.

Remember, what you do when there is nothing going on sets the tone for when your dog is around temptation. So, make sure that, as long as your dog knows the command, your dog performs the command if you ask for it.

One chance for the reward

We also don't repeat ourselves. If you do repeat your command endlessly, hoping the dog eventually does as he has been asked, it simply teaches the dog to ignore us and it devalues our authority. We give a command once and if the dog does it, we reward them (every time in the beginning), but if we give a command and the dog doesn't do it, we say 'No!' in a stern voice and repeat the command. Then we make it happen, but we don't reward.

The reasoning is that if we have to repeat ourselves, we don't reward because we want the dog to learn that following the command first time pays, whereas the second time is not fun, there's no reward, but you will have to follow the instruction anyway.

Now if we take 'Sit' as the example, we've given the command and the dog hasn't done it; we repeat one time and we will gently push the dog's bum down. Now if the dog then stays there for 5–10 seconds not moving, we can then start rewarding again so the dog knows it's that position that they get rewarded for.

A very simple rule to live by, guys, is if you ask for something then make it happen. If you've not released the dog from what you've asked it to do, the dog should still be doing it. The dog doesn't stop doing it until you release the dog or give them further instructions.

To release from 'Sit', when you want the dog to stop you can say 'Break' or 'Yes' or use your clicker. Further instructions could be 'Sit' and then 'Come' and then 'Sit' again; use your markers when you want or when the exercise is over.

Remember, guys, the less you say, the better. The more you repeat yourself the more you sound like someone nagging. Nobody wants that.

Commands

As mentioned previously, commands are something you ask the dog to do. The following are some of the commands all dogs should know, and some are life-saving.

Sit

This is one of the first basic and useful commands we teach – but sit must mean sit. Sit is so much more than just the action. It's the ability to hold that command until released, no matter what is going on. It can keep your dog calm; it can keep your dog safe. If your dog can sit and hold that sit, you can use it to help with dogs that lunge. If it's sitting as a dog passes it's not lunging. You can use it to help with jumping up too, and we will delve into this in more detail in later chapters. You will see how important this command is as we dig into more serious behaviour issues.

And remember guys, if you've asked the dog to sit and you haven't released it from that position or given further instructions and the dog isn't still in that sit, you're not being consistent. That dog had better go back into that sit.

How to teach 'Sit'

With a treat in your fingers, hold it to your dog's nose and slowly raise it above the dog's head. As the dog's head comes up, their bum naturally comes down. Once this happens, wait for them to make eye contact, say 'Yes' as the marker word and then step back and give the dog the treat.

Once your dog is fluid at this we can start to build a little bit of duration. Remember: sit means sit. So with the dog in the sit, you can count to three, say 'Good', using that marker, and give your dog a treat. Your dog should hold that position. Count to five, say 'Good', give your dog a treat. Now you're starting to build duration. Remember: if the dog breaks the sit at any time, simply pop the dog back into that sit. When looking to build some distance, for example a sit stay, where you want to move away from the dog, start very simple, have the dog in a sit, take one step back, use your marker 'Good', return to your dog, give him a treat. Then repeat, but take two steps back, going back to your dog; three steps, back to your dog; four steps, back to your dog; and so forth, until you've got a decent amount of distance.

Down

Just like sit, the down command is so important and, also like sit, the stay in down is implied. A dog must hold that down until released or he is given further instructions.

If your dog can hold a 'Down' anywhere, anytime, regardless of situation or distraction, you can take your dog virtually anywhere dogs are permitted. It will help them in pubs, restaurants and at friends' houses. You can use it to help a dog settle down. Down is so powerful if you are consistent with it.

But remember, guys, 'Down' means down until given further instructions.

How to teach 'Down'

With a treat in your fingers, hold it to your dog's nose and slowly bring the treat to the floor, until they are on the floor too. If you need to get their bum down that final bit, move the treat towards you. The moment all four legs and bum are down, say 'Yes' and reward your dog with the treat. Repeat this to reinforce the command.

To increase duration for down, use your 'Good' marker to build up time, just as you did with 'Sit'. When you have achieved a reasonable 'Down' duration, work in the 'Yes' marker so that the dog can come to you for the treat.

Leave it

This is life-saving and every dog needs to know this command. Your house is full of things you don't want your dog to eat, and so is the big wide world. What if your dog picks up a cooked chicken bone in a park, or something similar that could be life-threatening? Your dog needs to know 'Leave it' and leave whatever you ask it to, whether it's in its mouth or on the floor.

So many people miss this out or don't work on it enough and move on to teaching fancy tricks. Now I've got nothing against teaching your dog new tricks, but if you haven't taught them 'Leave it' (or other basic commands that can enrich and/or keep them safe) your priorities are mixed up.

If you have a dog that resource guards, this is also an important command, and we will dig deep into how to overcome resource guarding later in the book and how we will be adding this into the training.

How to teach 'Leave it'

I use two different methods for teaching 'Leave it'. One is with the dog on a lead and items on the floor and the other through playing tug or fetch. I like this second method, as the dog has the toy in its mouth, but both methods cover both scenarios where the dog might have to leave something, whether that thing is on the ground or already in its mouth.

Leave it #1: For this you'll need an everyday item your dog is not allowed. A kid's toy is a great example, maybe even a cuddly one that resembles a small furry animal, as that is *very* tempting! First ensure your dog is on a training lead, show them the toy, and then take the toy and throw it a short distance away from you, where it can still be seen. The dog's natural curiosity will mean it wants to go over and investigate. Use the lead to gently prevent this and say, 'Leave it'. When the lead goes slack, use the marker 'Yes' to reinforce that the dog has done as asked (when the dog is no longer pulling, he has effectively stopped trying to reach it) and reward.

I recommend you practise this a lot, with different items, in different rooms and at different times, to ensure the dog accepts the command applies to every situation and not just a particular one (that toy, that room, that time, etc.).

Leave it #2: This is another way to teach the 'Leave it' command. At SDT we use a tug rope, something the dog can bite on and play, and we have fun and off we go. I like to get the dog chasing the rope a bit and then let them grab it, have a right old tug and then stop the game completely, by saying 'Leave it' as you are holding the toy. You stop tugging so the game becomes boring, and when the dog lets go, you let them get straight back onto the toy and fun begins again.

You can repeat this method over and over until it's fluid.

If your dog is more ball-oriented, then use a two-ball method. Throw one ball and as the dog comes back, present ball number two and then use the 'Leave it' command. This nearly always gets the dog to drop the ball they have. Then throw the second ball. Rinse and repeat.

Practise 'Leave it' at random times, just as with method #1.

Heel

The 'Heel' command is part of lead walking and requires your dog to be calm and following you. For me, my only requirement for my dog on the lead is not to be pulling; I'm not expecting them to be walking exactly to my stride looking up at me the whole time. The 'Heel' command should only be taught once lead walking is working properly, at maybe about six months if you have a puppy. At this stage when you teach your dog to heel, you might like to do that for about 10 minutes of your walk, and then release it and allow it to sniff and explore as a reward for a job well done.

How to teach 'Heel'

Essentially, teaching your dog to heel simply requires that you only move forward when your dog isn't pulling. Doing anything else simply reinforces pulling. So, to teach 'Heel' you only walk forward when the lead is slack and there is no tension on the lead at all from your dog. When there is any tension, you stop.

When you feel the lead go slack, you mark and reward with 'Yes' and lure them to your left side with a treat and then continue to move forward. You will likely need to do this a lot, and it could take you ages to actually get anywhere. But this is a time when you need to put all thoughts of what it might look like, and how far you've actually got down the road, aside and focus on just getting it right – even if you get literally just a few steps.

It might be a painful process, but in the end, it works.

Thresholds

While not strictly a command as such, one thing you really need to teach your dog about is thresholds. When dog trainers say threshold training, what they mean is the behaviour you expect from your dog as a matter of good manners and safety when it passes through a threshold like a gate, door or entrance. Examples of this include your front door, your garden gate, the door to your dog's crate and your car boot.

When a dog crosses a threshold, it should be calm and waiting patiently; it should never rush out. This applies just as much to your garden as it does to your front door, because a dog that can't control itself at a threshold is in danger of running in front of a car, getting lost, or similar. It can be the cause of a tragedy.

As well as potentially avoiding an accident, threshold training sets the tone of what happens next. If a dog is going for a walk and it leaves the front door calmly, it sets the right tone; if it's going in the garden, working on thresholds will help them enter the garden calmly versus running out there barking its head off. Your dog should be calm when entering and exiting thresholds.

How to threshold train

First up, a safety must when you're training threshold. Make sure your dog is on a training or puppy lead, so if the dog fails, it is still safe.

To start, stand between your dog and the threshold – ideally this should be a back door onto a completely safe, enclosed area of your garden, say. Slowly open the threshold (the door or gate). If your dog moves forward, close it. Repeat. You need to do this until your dog stays in position while you open the door, and when the dog makes eye contact you move through the threshold with a release command (choose something like 'Let's go') and your dog follows.

To reinforce this command, as well as practising the above, you can also randomly open other doors without letting your dog pass through them.

CRATE TRAINING

Now crates are not cruel, they are not prison, so don't give me any of that 'How would you like it?' bollocks. In fact, I'd fucking love it. I'd love it if, after exercise, I could just switch off and relax. And, just to be clear, I'm not a dog. I don't sniff people's arses or piss in the garden. I don't cock my leg on lampposts, and I can't eat raw chicken. Your dog can and does, though. Basically, we're very different, so asking me if I'd like to be put in a crate is fucking pointless.

But as we love to compare dogs and children, let's look at it this way. We understand the importance of regular nap time for babies. We put them in cots to keep them safe and secure, we also use playpens with children. Now a crate is a cot for a dog; the only difference is it doesn't have unicorns painted on it – but if you want to make yourself feel better, by all means paint your crate or go to a company like PetPen UK who can make you a bespoke one.

Now we've got that out in the open, dogs need regular naps as a puppy and should be napping at certain times.

I recommend you put your dog in the crate for at least one to two hours after exercise so they can switch off. If you crate your dog when you are eating, when the kids are eating, or any time when food is around, you will also have a much calmer dog at these times, not begging or stealing food.

You won't have to do this forever, guys. Once your dog has learnt to switch off in the crate you can use a dog bed or a spot on the sofa, but having used a crate to begin with, it will be much easier to teach as you have created a pattern of behaviour that will become second nature to the dog. Dogs that have separation anxiety, dogs that bark at every single noise, dogs that terrorise you and your children are very rarely crate trained and don't have an off switch.

The basics

Before we start, a word about safety. To keep your dog safe you must check the positioning of your crate to ensure it's not too hot (i.e. next to a hot radiator or in direct sun), that any covering you've used still allows plenty of ventilation, and that you have removed any collar or lead your dog may be wearing (these can go on as the dog leaves the crate, especially if you're having problems with an overexcitable puppy).

In terms of how long you can keep your dog in a crate, it would never be longer than four hours, and if it's a young puppy that's still learning to control its bladder, then it would be a lot, lot shorter (maybe an hour). If a dog is messing inside its crate, you've gone badly wrong. A quick word on crating your dog overnight, it's fine to leave your dog in the crate overnight while you sleep, providing the dog has full bladder control. Ideally, where possible, it's always best to tire your pup out before you pop him in the crate, so they switch off quicker. This is especially true in the mornings if you're heading off to work, as the dog has only just got up from sleeping all night and needs some stimulation.

If there's an emergency – and we're talking the serious type such as needing to go to hospital, etc. – then occasionally spending longer in the crate is okay. But if you're regularly out of the house for, say, eight hours a day, you need to consider alternative arrangements. Get yourself a decent dog walker to break up your dog's day with an hour's walk after four hours of crate time. (I don't recommend 'doggy daycare'.)

Also, remember that a crate should never be used as a punishment, a place where you put your dog out of sheer frustration. If you do this, you'll be creating negative associations that will ruin any further training with the crate. The idea of the crate is for it to become the dog's safe space, a place they can go to to relax and switch off. It should never be a place that they fear.

Crating a young puppy

With a puppy that's maybe eight to ten weeks old, you'll be looking at no more than one to two hours in a crate. If they're still teething, you can place a bone or a Kong inside with them. To start with, to get them used to the idea that the crate is a safe, happy place, think in terms of about 30–60 minutes outside the crate, during which time you'll be interacting with and training them, and then back in for a nap. You can gradually increase both the time in the crate and the time out of the crate as they develop. Expect to get up in the night for a pup, just as you would for a baby human. Only when a dog has full bladder control can you consider crating for longer, say up to four hours.

Getting your dog used to the crate

How To Train Your Dog

'Password: SDTBook'

To start crate training you'll need your dog's favourite treats. Show them the treats and get them interested. Throw some treats deep into the crate and say 'Crate' so the dog follows the food in, snuffles to find the treats, and then, when the dog's attention returns to you, use a marker word such as 'Yes' for the dog to come out again and receive another treat. Your aim to is get your dog to go happily into the crate.

Do this over and over, keeping it rewarding for your dog, and then gradually build up the time the dog is in the crate. Work up to closing the door between the dog going in and coming out, and then to walking away out of the room too. The key here is to build a positive association with the crate in your dog's head. That's why you need to work on it as if it's a training game. You can also feed your dog through the bars of the crate when they are inside to increase the feel-good factor.

It's also important to ensure a calm exit, so only open the door to release if the dog is calm (not rushing). For an overexcited dog, consider popping on a lead as they come out. A lead can be useful to encourage a reluctant dog into the crate too.

Crate training is non-negotiable, so make sure this fun game of in/out is one of the first things you tackle.

> **QUICK CRATE HACK**
>
> If your dog doesn't settle when in the crate, a good hack is to cover up the crate but leave a small 'window' at the bottom of it. This will mean your dog has to lie down to be able to see out, and once it is lying down, it starts to relax much quicker.

Moving on from the crate

This is likely your final goal, but it's not necessarily an age thing, although many puppies may be ready from ten months to a year. It's more about judging when it's safe for your dog to be given the run of the house/room. If they're teething, which can still happen way into adolescence (which kicks in at around six months), it's likely they might still be at risk of chewing something not designed to be chewed (electrical wires, furniture, shoes). But if your dog is toilet trained, knows how to settle and is not destructive in any way, then it's likely ready for a bit more freedom.

Some dogs may never be ready. My late dog Sammie was still crated whenever we left the house. There were several reasons: one is that she loved to chew Barbie dolls, which my kids love to leave out; and the other is that she didn't like loud bangs, which we have locally. She instinctively felt safer in her crate because of this. Roxy, my other dog, by comparison, is not crated when we leave. Different dogs, different needs.

Either way, it's a mistake to stop using the crate too soon, so don't rush that.

A LITTLE REMINDER

As mentioned in threshold training (p.59), for safety, the teaching of commands is best done using a puppy or training lead. If your dog still has a way to go before it is reliably following commands, or you are teaching something for the first time, use an indoor training lead to maintain control. This type of lead is thin and lightweight, almost ribbon-like. About 10 to 15 feet long, there's no handle at the end so there's no risk it could get caught on something. In fact, it's a misconception that leads are only for use outside the home and, if you're still training, this type of lead can go on your dog once it comes out of the crate to help you both stay safe.

IS MY DOG A DICK?

In the next chapters, we'll move on to tackle those serious issues you might be having indoors and out. But before we do, it's important to talk about alternative behaviours, or why your dog might seem to be misbehaving in the first place.

Just bear in mind, many times your dog is misbehaving not to be a dick but simply because he doesn't know what you want him to do, because you haven't shown him. For example, your dog might be jumping up because he gets attention for doing it. You might not realise that instead of jumping up, performing a sit is what could get him the attention he wants, because you've not taught him that. Maybe your dog is running into the garden barking every time you let them out, but you've not shown them what you want them to do instead.

So next time your dog is misbehaving, ask yourself, what do I want them to do instead? What could I add or teach right now that could benefit my dog, that would be a better behaviour than what he's doing? Or ask yourself, does my dog even know what I want him to do? Making sure you show the dog what you want, and rewarding what you want, goes a long, long way.

The golden rule at SDT is:

If you like it, fuss it, love it, reward it.

And if you don't, show them what you want them to do instead, so you can fuss it, love it, reward it.

Now let's get this party started!!!

TAKEAWAYS

- Every dog should know the basic commands of 'Sit', 'Down', 'Leave it' and 'Heel'
- Effective dog training is built on getting and keeping your dog's attention/focus on you

- Markers are key words that indicate a dog has done what you've asked, or is doing what you've asked and that there is a reward to follow.
- 'Yes', 'Good' and 'Break' are the markers we use
- A clicker can be used as a marker
- Threshold training is essential and can save your dog's life; dogs must never rush through or across thresholds such as doors and gates
- Correct crate training helps with all your other training, giving the dog a safe, switch-off space
- Crate training is non-negotiable and should start right away
- A crate should never be used as a punishment
- A crate will keep your dog safe and can be comforting to a dog that may be anxious
- Make crate training into a fun game to build positive associations
- A dog that is still in training should always be on a puppy training lead for safety purposes
- If your dog is misbehaving, ask yourself what you want them to do instead

PART II
YOUR DOG INDOORS

CHAPTER 6

Behavioural problems at home

This chapter covers the most common behavioural problems that affect dogs when they are inside the home. Now before we dig deep into those individual issues, I want to remind you: if you are strict with the three core principles I outlined earlier, and your training foundations are in place, any problems – inside the home or out – will be massively reduced. Those approaches go a long way to helping you have the dog you want.

A lot of people will excuse minor behaviour lapses inside the home, or even think certain things are not that important, like the dog not coming to you the first time you call it in from the garden or another room, for example. But let me tell you, problems start at home. If your dog can ignore you, get away with stuff, or even practise bad behaviour such as reactivity in the home, this will directly impact how the dog behaves when it is outside the home. Remember: the home is the safe space and has next to no distractions. If problems in the home are not addressed, the real world will be much harder.

If your dog has problems in the house, it should be on an indoor training lead. This allows you to lead your dog out of trouble conflict-free and gives you more control. Indoor leads should be thin and lightweight, with no handle that could snag on things.

So, let's begin.

EXCESSIVE BARKING

If your dog is barking at every sound it hears, barking for attention, or is showing any form of over-the-top barking, this can often stem from not getting enough exercise and not enough down time. Think about it this way: if a dog isn't sleeping enough because it's not tired or there's not enough forced nap time, it will be up and down like a yo-yo. This means lots of broken sleep and often this leads to anxiety-based behaviours, such as excessive barking.

Making sure we follow the three core principles of Exercise, Diet and Off Switch will mean such behaviour is less likely.

The other thing to do, and it's ideally best done when your dog is a puppy, is that when the dog is sleeping, that's the time to do housework or things for yourself. Don't tiptoe around trying not to make a sound. Behave as normal, making the kind of noises that would be normal. This way we don't end up with sound-sensitive dogs that bark at every noise they hear.

If a dog is barking in the garden and, every time you open the back door, they go racing to the end of the garden making a noise, things need to change. Don't make the mistake of letting the dog repeat the same thing over and over by opening the door and letting your dog out to do as he pleases. Instead, work on those thresholds we spoke about earlier and wait for the dog to be calm at the back door before you allow him to exit. Take the dog in the garden on a lead for a couple of weeks to change the pattern of behaviour and instead form a new way of behaving. Basically, if your dog is barking at something and you want to change that, ask yourself what you would like them to do instead, and show them.

Now let's talk about the other forms of reactivity we often get called to help with at SDT.

REACTIVITY TO THE DOORBELL

Dogs barking when the doorbell goes is normal and we don't mind this – it's a good deterrent and it's natural for some alert barking from a dog. However, it is problematic if we can't stop the barking, or if the noise continues well after the visitor has come into the house.

What I like to do here is teach my dog what the doorbell means. The doorbell is a sound that the dog builds an association with, just like the clicker. But unlike the clicker that leads to a reward for a lot of dogs, to a dog that won't stop barking the doorbell means 'LET'S GO FUCKING MENTAL!' So, we want to change this, and this is how we do it.

First up, put the dog on an indoor training lead (remember, this is essential if the dog has problems inside). I like to sit down, relax and play the Ring doorbell sound from my phone. You can also play doorbell sounds on YouTube or get a friend to stand outside your front door and ring the doorbell repeatedly. This sound alone will often make the dog go running to the door barking. Let that happen and get up as normal and go to the door. Then I pick up the lead and stand between the dog and the front door and I say, 'Enough'. I wait until the dog stops barking and then reward the dog. Next, I place the dog in a sit, making sure I can reach the door handle and that I'm between the dog and the door, and with the dog in a sit and not barking I open the door. If the dog comes out of the sit, I simply pull up on the lead and place them back into a sit. I practise this over and over, at random times, and when I'm in different rooms of the house, so it becomes normal. I don't just wait for someone to ring the doorbell for me to practise the approach.

A good little tip you can use to practise real-life situations is to get any family members who would usually use a key to enter the house to ring the doorbell instead when they come home. Remind family and friends that come over that they will need to be patient when they ring the bell as it's important to not rush opening the door. The dog must always be calm before the door opens, and in a sit. Remember: what takes a long time at first gets quicker every time if you are consistent.

Eventually, through repetitions, the dog will know what to do when the door goes; the doorbell is now a positive, the dog has done its job, and you will take it from there. The process is organised and structured and this is vital for the next problem we are about to address.

REACTIVITY TO VISITORS

Now this is such a common issue, especially for those

dogs that were bought as puppies during lockdown because they were never exposed to people coming and going when they were young. It's also one of those areas where *you* need to be calm and confident, because if the dog senses you are worried when people come round – even though it's not the people you are worried about – your dog builds the association that people coming into the house makes mum/dad scared, and then the dog sees them as a threat.

We also need to make sure that people who come round listen to us and follow our instructions. This even applies to those people that have had dogs their whole life or think they know better than you! You do what's best for your dog and follow these instructions. And if they can't respect that, do you really want them in your house?

The very first step in fixing this problem is to make sure we've done doorbell training. This helps tenfold as we've already taken the time to build a positive association with the door and not linked it with tension or a 'bad thing' generally. Then, when that doorbell does go, you calmly and patiently pick up the training lead on your dog and make sure the dog is behind you, not in front of you, and that all is calm and quiet before you open the door.

When you open the door, move back a bit and create more space. Tell your guests to act as if you don't have a dog – no staring, no talking, no holding a hand out for the dog to sniff. This part is so important to follow. If someone tries to force themselves on the dog when he doesn't want that, the dog knows the person doesn't understand them, and it ruins the trust, making the reactivity worse. In order to truly help a dog trust the visitor, he needs to be ignored so he learns nothing bad is going to happen.

Now, back to the door opening and people coming in. Tell your guests to ignore the dog but sweeten the deal (for your dog) by having a jar of treats by the front door. Get the visitors to take a handful of treats and throw them over your dog's head (remember, your dog should be behind you at this point). By throwing the treats over your dog's head your guests are creating space, and it is easier for your dog to get them. Now your dog has a positive association to that person, who hasn't forced them to come close to them to get a treat (if your guest had held the treat in their hand, your dog would have been forced to come closer to take it).

Why does this work?

In the past, people were often told to hold out a treat for a nervous dog to come and take. But for a nervous and/or reactive dog, coming to you to take it from your hand sets off conflicting instincts. The first reason for this is that when a dog gets nervous it often isn't using its nose but its eyes. Holding out a hand for the dog to sniff or to offer a treat can often be mistaken as you reaching out to touch the dog, which can trigger a reaction. That can trigger a reaction. Even a dog that has been brave enough to come and take the treat can quickly panic and retreat as it gets closer, and potentially react.

Instead, when we throw the treat we are giving the dog space, which is key for a reactive and nervous dog to feel comfortable. When we throw the treats over the dog's head, we've created a positive-only association as there's no need to approach the scary thing to get the reward. As the dog snuffles for the treat, the nose becomes engaged, and using his nose automatically relaxes a dog. Your guests should now go into the main room of the house and behave normally. Note that you still have hold of the dog's lead at this stage, and you can continue to throw treats to build up the dog's confidence.

If your dog is nervous but not reactive, you can let the dog go over to the person to sniff but, again, *no touching, no talking, no staring and no holding hands out.* Here your aim is for the dog to be able to sniff on his terms, as using his nose is what will help the dog relax and gather information. Sniffing is a ritual that you must let the dog complete; when it's done the dog will either walk away, which means it's not interested in the person, or the dog will sit and present itself to your guest. If the dog does the latter then your visitor can offer a treat with their hand low by their side, but I would avoid stroking for the first visit or two so the dog gets to know the person better.

If the dog has a history of lunging at guests, to avoid any upset it's best not to let him go over to sniff newcomers on their first visit. Just the presence of the person who is following the rules outlined above and creating a positive association will have a lasting impact. On the next visit you should be able to move on to the sniffing stage. Once the dog has seen the person and you've followed all the above, you can either keep the dog on the lead next to you or send it to its crate to switch off, preferably with the crate in the room where you guys all are during these visits.

What not to do

Don't put a dog in his crate or shut the dog away when the door goes, or when someone arrives. This can often make the behaviour worse because your dog is scared and then it gets shut away with no direction. If the dog is shut away, it knows someone new is there but can't see for himself. Instead, we use leads (and muzzles as necessary) so the dog can learn to be a part of the action before being instructed to settle down.

However, even when a dog has settled down you need to be mindful. The two times a dog is likely to react the most to visitors is when they first come in and when the dog finally relaxes and goes to sleep, and then someone moves. To help this, whenever a guest is going to move, we simply throw a treat at the dog or into the crate (depending on where the dog is) or give the treat yourself. This helps form a positive association, that people moving around is a good thing.

Guys, getting a dog used to someone new coming into the home is a bit like dating. Have your guest play hard to get; don't give it to them all on the first date, leave the dog wanting more. Don't rush or force the relationship, just enjoy the process. The more times the dog sees that person, the easier it gets.

JUMPING UP

Sometimes guests arriving doesn't make the dog nervous or reactive, but the exact opposite: the dog goes nuts! Dogs jumping up is such a common issue, and it's one of the questions we get asked loads, but there is such a simple fix if you are consistent with how you handle this.

Jumping up normally starts from puppyhood, when the puppy is small and cute and often gets rewarded for the behaviour. But when it gets bigger, suddenly it's a problem. This is why it's so important when you get a dog to start as you mean to go on. Another common reason for jumping up is excitement – the more excited the dog gets, the harder it finds it to control itself, especially if it has poor impulse control. So, I'm going to break jumping up into two categories: the first will be jumping up at you guys, the owners, and the second jumping up at guests.

Jumping up at you

We're working on this first because we are meant to lead by example. Many times, if your dog can do something to or with you, it will do the same to someone else. With that in mind it's important to make sure we are leading by example because even if you don't mind it, we would hate for the dog to jump up and hurt or scare an elderly person or a child.

So how do we address jumping up at you? First, we make sure that before we stroke the dog, it is doing something we like. Unless we are already cuddled on the sofa, I like to ask the dog to sit before I stroke them. I also make sure I ask the dog to sit before giving it a treat and before food, so the dog learns this is the behaviour that gets them good things. If we are consistent with this, you will find the dog will start to sit for a fuss rather than jumping up for a fuss. Sit, stroke. Sit, stroke. Sit, stroke. Drum it in, make it a way of life, make it the good habit you form.

Now remember that training lead I like you to keep on? This is another way it will come in handy. If the dog jumps up, you can use the lead to get the dog off; give a sharp tug up on it and then ask for a sit instead. Rinse and repeat.

What about if your dog is jumping up at you when you first come home? If this is the case, walk straight past your dog, don't say a word to it, greet your family, unload the shopping, put the kettle on, do whatever it is you're doing, and wait for a bit of calmness. When your dog is calm, ask for a sit and calmly stroke your dog. And no, it's not cruel to ignore the dog, even if you are the only human member in the household. It is cruel to come in, hype the dog up and then moan when it jumps up. Put the needs of the dog first and show him what's expected before fulfilling your need to stroke and interact with the dog. Otherwise, the overexcited way you've allowed the dog to greet you (and be rewarded for it) will spill over to other guests like poor old grandma.

Remember, you won't have to do this forever. When the new pattern of behaviour is formed, your dog will quickly start behaving calmly when you come home, straight away coming over with a sit that you can reward. So, what takes a few minutes to begin with will soon take a few seconds, if we are consistent over time.

Jumping up at guests

This is an easier problem to solve if you've already followed the doorbell advice (p.73), as we take a very similar approach to what you do if you have a reactive dog and people come over. First, we make sure the dog is calm before we open the door, then we make sure the guests ignore the dog completely, and then if our dog is calm and waits for permission to go over to the person, we can allow them to do so. The reason guests should ignore your friendly dog, just as they would a more reactive one, is because human speech often creates excitement and can make the dog jump up. And we want that nose engaged, not the ears. We want the dog to sniff the new person – and finish sniffing – before any physical or verbal interaction takes place. And just as a reminder, you should still be holding on to the training lead.

Now when the dog finishes sniffing, it might walk away – a sign that it's not that into you. But if the dog offers himself to you, by way of a nudge or sitting, or even presenting its backside, then it generally wants attention, so instruct your guests to first ask the dog to sit (remember: sit, stroke, sit, stroke) and calmly stroke the dog, almost like a massage. If the dog jumps up, the fuss stops, you intervene, and we rinse and repeat as needed every time the dog is calm for as long as you or your guest wants to.

Always remember how important that nose is to dogs, guys. Sniffing is the way dogs greet, so let the dog have a good sniff. Often, when that nose is engaged the dog is calm and behaving naturally, so always instruct guests to let the dog do this natural behaviour before interaction. Dogs are nose, eyes, ears in that order. Do not activate the ears by talking, or the eyes through trying to touch, before the dog has had a chance to sniff. You'll learn more about the importance of sniffing when we tackle outside issues later.

WINDOW BARKING

Barking wildly when anything passes by the window is an issue in a lot of houses but it's a relatively easy one to fix. First, make sure the three core principles are in place, so our dogs don't have pent-up energy to expend, and they are more inclined to chill out at home. We must also avoid the dogs getting into the habit of watching the world go by. If a dog is sitting on the couch looking out the window and then barking, off the couch it goes. If there's any barking the dog gets off the sofa. When the dog is calm you can invite them back up. Very quickly the dog will learn to stop barking because it means they have to get off the sofa.

If it's a small dog that likes to sit on the back of the sofa, but that sofa happens to be by the window, you can either a) stop letting the dog on the back of the sofa, period, or b) move the sofa so when the dog is on the back, it's not able to look out of the window. Make sure you follow the rules in the excessive barking section too (p.72), as that will also help massively with this. Also remember that if the dog can practise reactivity in the house, it can often manifest when it's outside too.

Certain breeds are more likely to bark in the home, such as guarding breeds like German Shepherds and Rottweilers, and small dogs like Chihuahuas and Dachshunds are also very good watch dogs that will bark at subtle noises. It's worth bearing that in mind if you are thinking of adding another dog into the mix.

REACTIVITY TO THE TV

This is an issue I see with some dogs, and for some reason I see it most with Pugs, Rottweilers and terrier breeds. But it's not exclusive to them, and any dog can develop this issue. Sorting it doesn't have to be stressful and we deal with it by turning it into a game.

At home, with your dog on its training lead, take their dinner bowl or a few reward treats and sit down. Place your dog in a 'Down' at your feet and step on the lead. You want a short lead but not so short it's forcing the dog down, but just short enough that if the dog runs it will quickly hit the end of the lead. (You can use a harness for this if you want.) Next, put some animal programmes on the television...and wait.

When your dog sees an animal it's likely to go running and start barking – but wait! Something happened. The dog just hit the end of the lead and that interrupts the dog, so he looks back to see what just happened. At this moment you give a firm 'Enough' and place the dog back into a 'Down'. Remember: you don't reward here, because the dog didn't stay in the 'Down' position. If you dish out treats here, you're encouraging the dog to break position.

Now the next time your dog sees an animal on the telly, because of what just happened he should look at the TV but then look at you. We then mark this behaviour and reward the dog. Rinse and repeat. I recommend short sessions reinforcing this in the beginning so as not to overwhelm the dog.

ACCIDENTS VS SCENT MARKING

If your dog has full bladder control and is suddenly peeing on everything in the house this generally isn't an accident, but more to do with the dog marking its territory. It's different from having an accident and we often see this around the adolescent stage from six to eight months onwards.

True accidents, however, usually occur when you're not there, or at more random times. There is often a pattern to the behaviour too, which you can work out if you sit down and look at when it's happening. Sometimes it's overnight, sometimes it's when you've been out for the day. Marking is different and is often performed on new things, like rugs, furniture, bags and shoes, etc. Journalling might help you spot patterns like this.

First let's tackle accidents in the house. The three core principles pretty much will stop this. A decent diet is key; remember, if the dog is on a diet that's not agreeing with it, it's going to drink more and thus end up peeing more. It can also affect bowel movements and make them uncontrollable. Lack of exercise and proper routine can also be contributing factors, as well as health. So, if the dog is on a decent diet, has enough stimulating exercise and has a routine, and it's still having accidents, then it could be a health problem you need to look into. You should consider a vet check to rule out physical problems.

But if they are having accidents, a physical cause has been ruled out and it's not marking, I suggest you go right back to basics. Absolutely *no* use of puppy pads, since that can give a dog the idea messing inside is acceptable.

Instead, keep them on a training lead when indoors, take them outside, wait for them to do their business, give them a treat, make a fuss and use your command like 'Go toilet'.

Marking in the house nearly always happens when the dog has no rules or boundaries in place, i.e., when there is no routine, no forced nap time, when it is allowed on the sofa when it feels like without being invited, takes things it shouldn't, has free access to toys all the time, and demands attention constantly on its own terms. You will also see marking more often in multi-dog households when there are no rules between the dogs, and they begin to mark their territory.

So how do we stop this? We use an indoor lead, we have a routine, we don't negotiate with the dog, and when we ask the dog to do something, it does it first time or we make it happen. We don't give the dog the full run of the house straight away; we restrict their freedom to access certain rooms, certain items and spaces until they have been taught to behave properly, and then we gradually allow more freedom. We make sure fuss is on our terms, we make them work for it, as well as for food and attention, and very quickly the dogs realise that all good things come from us. We are calm, we are confident. The dog follows us and will stop the marking behaviour.

Now I know some of you might think, that's a military boot camp you are running there, but remember, guys, leave your emotions at the door. Having a puppy is very similar to having a toddler. Would you leave a toddler unsupervised? Would you leave things that could be dangerous lying around for a toddler to pick up? Do you allow your toddler the same freedom as your teenagers? No, you don't – and if you do, it will cause problems. Puppies need structure to learn how to behave and to be safe, and if they don't get it as a puppy, they won't magically grow out of bad behaviour. It's more likely just to get worse; so often, if they haven't been taught it as a puppy, we must do some puppy foundation stuff with an older dog.

If we take the time to meet the needs of the dog and raise them the right way, we reduce the chances of serious issues developing. My final point on this matter is that dogs love structure and working for things, for example sitting before a fuss, waiting to be asked to do something, behaving a certain way before leaving the house, knowing what they can do and what they can't do – this builds their confidence. Yes, it seems like a lot of rules, but very quickly you will see it's not and it will become second nature. All we are doing is giving more access to fun stuff as and when the dog is ready and behaved.

STEALING THINGS

Now, just like marking, dogs will steal things when they haven't been taught how to behave. At the end of the day dogs are opportunistic. And if it's fun or rewarding for them, they are likely to do it, even if it's not fun for us. If they can, they will. So, again, right at the beginning we need to make sure we always know where the dog is, and we make it less likely they'll steal tempting stuff by not leaving it around. Treat your dog like a toddler in the beginning and imagine everything you don't want the dog to pick up is a choking hazard. Very quickly you will stop leaving things lying around. Likewise, don't leave your dinner on the table when you are out of the room.

To avoid your dog taking children's toys from your kids when the kids are playing, teach your dog what to do instead at such times. For example, you could practise 'Down' stays. Provide dog toys for doggy playtime with you or the kids, and then move to rest time, so they don't need to go round stealing what's not theirs. Crate when you're eating so the dog learns what to do when it's your mealtime. Appropriate behaviour then becomes second nature. Only allow free roaming when your dog is trained and knows 'Leave it', which is one of the most valuable and life-saving commands. Only then is it ready for more freedom.

RESOURCE GUARDING

While stealing shoes or a child's toy here and there might not seem like a big deal, aside from the harm it could do the dog or your possessions, a real problem that can quickly develop from dogs stealing things is resource guarding.

Resource guarding (RG) is when a dog has an item or something they view as valuable (the resource) and refuses to give it up and shows signs of aggression when you try to take it. RG can be shown towards people or towards other animals and can affect any dog, of any breed of virtually any age. In my experience it is most prevalent with spaniels, especially the Cocker Spaniel, and terriers. We'll talk about resource guarding with food later, but to begin with we'll tackle the guarding of toys and other items such as sofas and even people.

RG begins when a dog steals something over and over and then gets fed up with you, or another animal, taking it away from them. So, it's important that we really take in what we discussed when it comes to stealing things. If a dog guards any item from you, the handler, it loses that item. If it's the sofa, they lose that; if it's toys, they lose them. We are extra strict with dogs that steal things that have RG. We implement a 'prison phase' system for them (this is also implemented with food aggression, and there'll be more on that shortly).

The prison phase system is where your dog always goes in its crate or a pen when it's unattended. They go in it for a couple of hours at a time. When they come out, they come out on a lead, and you hold that lead. You work on your training with the dog, on your foundations and relationship, and you incorporate 'Leave it' – but *not* via a tug-of-war game (look back at the 'Leave it' section on p.56). You use 'Leave it' with the dog on the lead after a vigorous training session or play session and then you can chill out with your dog on the sofa (as long as it's not guarding that) or on the floor working on 'Down', and then it's back in the crate. Repeat this routine for a week. After a week of intense training, you can slowly introduce the items that have become problematic again, increase the time spent out of the crate on a lead, and start to allow more leeway. By this time 'Leave it' should be more bombproof, and the dog's listening will be stronger. You can try to introduce toys again, such as balls, but never leave the dog to its own devices with them.

If it's the sofa that the dog is guarding, you can start to invite them on it for short periods of time. Using a training lead, I would also have the dog get off the sofa every time a human goes to sit down and then wait to be invited back on. This means, if the dog is on the sofa with you, and your partner walks towards the sofa, you or your partner gets the dog off the sofa, and then once you're both comfortably seated, you invite the dog back on. This will also help if the dog guards you on the sofa from other family members. Another example is if the dog is on the sofa and you get up, perhaps to make a coffee; when you walk back into the room, get the dog off the sofa before you sit down, and then invite the dog back on the sofa with you.

If the resource the dog is guarding is you, then separation is required. Don't let the dog follow you from room to room for a bit. Don't let the dog sit in front of you by your feet. Similarly, don't have the dog in front of you if people outside the house approach you. Instead, teach your dog this 'Away' game for people who approach you in the house. The Away game is simple: you say 'Away' and throw a treat, which gets the dog to move away to get it. (You can do this if you are at home and the dog has sat next to you when you didn't want it to.) Send it 'Away' and have the other person come towards you. This command can also come in handy in other areas.

You also need to make sure that you are not creating a needy dog, because dogs that resource guard their owners can often have separation anxiety from them as well. A lot of the same rules – such as not fussing the dog when it's being needy, not letting the dog follow you from room to room, and teaching the dog to spend short periods of time by itself – need to be applied to a dog that has separation anxiety. (There's more on separation anxiety in the next chapter.)

Growling or food aggression?

Before we talk about food aggression in detail, let's just talk about dogs guarding items from other dogs. There is a massive difference between a dog growling because another dog is trying to take what they have, and a dog going to attack another just for being close to them when they have something of value.

If your dog has something and another dog wants it, and it's been nice enough to let you know with a growl it's not happy, then don't punish your dog. Instead advocate for your dog; don't let other dogs invade your dog's personal space when it has something. But if your dog goes to attack another dog for being near it, even if the second dog isn't showing any interest in what is being guarded, then it's time to remove that toy or item.

The resource guarding dog should also be muzzled in public when other animals are around until further training has been carried out. If it's in the home then make sure they have their own space (we discuss the multi-dog household in Chapter 8), and make sure there are rules to cover everything like play, sofas, food, toys and fuss.

So, is it okay for dogs to growl or should we correct it? This is not a black-and-white area; in fact, context is everything here. Growling by itself is simply a way of communicating for dogs. Dogs will growl when they are happy, some will growl during play with you or with other dogs, and a lot of the time growls are okay. But because the context that a growl has happened in is so important, it isn't necessarily best covered in a book. If you're in doubt about how serious or dangerous your dog's growling is, it's better addressed in person, with a decent trainer.

Now my late Staffie, Sammie, was bombproof with other dogs, so if she was growling at a dog I would thank her, because it meant the dog was being rude or pushy, and it was my cue to step in and advocate for her. Her growling was a warning, but since I then took over the situation, she didn't escalate her behaviour or feel the need to have to deal with it by herself. This is a growl that I'm thankful for.

My little Roxy the rescue, on the other hand, had resource guarding issues with toys if other dogs were involved. When we got her, she came into a home with two other dogs and she would growl if she had something and Sammie or Daisy walked into the room, even if they were nowhere near her. This is an unacceptable growl that I would correct because she's overreacting to nothing, and it needs nipping in the bud. I address a growl that is an overreaction by holding the dog accountable, but if a growl is because someone is doing something that's rude or pushy towards my dogs, be it human or dog, I correct that human or dog, so my dog doesn't have to. In that way, they trust I will keep them safe.

Food aggression

Dealing with this problem requires a very similar technique to implementing the 'prison phase' system (p.88). But we also make sure we hand feed, and that's non-negotiable. No more food bowl for a while. All food comes from your hand and is a reward for the dog doing something you've asked it to do. You also work on 'Leave it' and other training, just like in the prison phase. After a week you can reintroduce the food bowl but with strict rules.

And those rules are:

- While the food is being prepared, the dog is in its crate.
- Once food is prepared, the food bowl is left on the side as you get the dog.
- Your dog must be calm before you open the crate door, and its lead must be attached before letting the dog out of the crate fully.
- You then walk into the kitchen, place the dog in a 'Sit' and go to pick up the bowl.
- If the dog moves out of the sit, the bowl goes back and the dog goes back into a sit.
- You must be able to put the bowl down and then release the dog from its sit.
- Place the bowl on some kind of raised platform, so the dog doesn't stand right over it in a guarding position.

- Once the dog starts eating, drop some tasty treat like chicken into the bowl and walk away.
- Repeat this process for the next few days, walking away and walking towards the dog while he is eating, but never asking for anything, just dropping high-value treats which shows the dog that you walking towards him isn't a threat.

Now I do recommend that you get a trainer into the home, especially if it's a dog that is capable of hospitalising you and/or is one that has bitten over resources. We offer home visits for these very issues, and this is the safest way of dealing with serious food aggression.

DESTRUCTIVE BEHAVIOUR

Destructive behaviour in the house is often the result of boredom, just like stealing things. Remember: that energy must go somewhere guys, whether you like it or not. To prevent destructive behaviour, you must make sure that you are exercising your dog properly and teaching the off switch. Dogs that are happy and content won't be bored. We also want to make sure that when the dog is away from its crate, we are training with them, having fun with them, or providing something to keep them occupied, like a licky mat, Kong or brain puzzle, or even a juicy bone. Keep interactive toys like balls or tug toys just for when you are playing with the dog. If these things aren't left lying around, they have more meaning to the dog when you present them. Teething puppies will also chew everything, so the above will help them also.

DOGS ON THE SOFA, YES OR NO?

I have no objections to dogs being on the sofa whatsoever, if they behave and wait to be invited. I tend to encourage this more once a dog has learnt to settle in its crate. Sofas are a great place to sit and snuggle with the dog as you are chilling out. The only dogs that I don't let on the sofa are dogs who think it's a play gym, and dogs who guard the sofa or people until training has been completed (see Resource Guarding on p.87). If a dog jumps on the sofa without permission I get them straight off. I want them to wait calmly for me to invite them before they get on. I also don't fuss the dog or give them any attention when I first invite them up until they are lying down and we are comfy, so the dog learns that getting up and settled is what gets them the attention. Be strict with this, especially if you have behaviour problems and/or a multi-dog household. Any messing around on the sofa, it's off the sofa you go. Rinse and repeat until the dog gets the memo.

PLAYING IN THE HOUSE

I don't encourage this really, because the house is not a play area. Dogs can play in the garden and play on walks – that's what walk time is all about, learning, playing, bonding. If you have two dogs and they want to play, take them outside and supervise. If you want to play with your dog, take it outside. If it's raining, suck it up; dogs still need to go outside when it's raining. The only thing I give dogs in the house to keep them amused is a bone, a Kong, or a puzzle from time to time. The rest of the time, if you are doing everything correctly, your dog won't need to be running around the house as it will be tired from the long walks and activities you do outside.

FIREWORKS AND THUNDERSTORMS

Fireworks and thunderstorms can be stressful times for our four-legged friends. But if you don't have any issues here, don't create ones by worrying that this will be the year your dog reacts to fireworks. If there are no problems, don't go looking for them.

Once upon a time I had three dogs. Cancer has since got two of them, Daisy and Sammie. Little Roxy is still going strong – got to love those terriers! Out of the three, Daisy was the only one who never had an issue with fireworks, and that's because we never made a big deal about them. But Sammie and Roxy were both rescues and the damage had already been done by the time they came to me.

What I find is best for many dogs that do have problems with loud noises such as thunder or fireworks is simply using their crate. That's right, the crate. Put the crate in the same room as you, and if you've conditioned your dog to the crate and used it correctly, it is your dog's safe space. Whenever it's firework season and the fireworks start going off, Roxy goes into the crate and gets a juicy beef trachea to keep her occupied. By the time she's done with that, she's sleeping and not fazed by the bangs. But if you leave her to her own devices, she paces and shakes and gets stressed by the noise. The crate is a game-changer.

Now really the crate is just one part of the strategy. Before fireworks are due to go off, or a thunderstorm is approaching, I always make sure that we go for a nice long walk, sometimes double the amount of time we normally would. This makes her doubly tired. A tired dog is much more likely to relax. I also turn the TV up louder than normal, draw the curtains and then carry on my business as normal to keep to a familiar routine, which can provide security. I also bust out the lavender-scented candles as they have a calming effect on dogs. That's all I need to do with Roxy.

Some dogs might feel happier on the sofa next to you – if they do, that's fine, you can even give them a massage at this time; just don't sit there feeling sorry for them or freaking out, as they will freak out more. But if the dog is restless then their crate is best.

Thunder jackets

Thunder jackets can also be a game-changer. I've not needed to use one for my dogs, but I have recommended them to a lot of people over the years to help with reactivity to noise. A thunder jacket is a jacket that goes on the dog and does up tightly, as the feeling of being constricted can help a dog relax. The big mistake when using thunder jackets is that people don't do them up tight enough so it's just like a dog wearing a normal jacket, and that won't help a great deal for this problem.

Playing classical music can help massively too, but remember you must play it at random times so the dog doesn't associate it with specific events like fireworks and thunder. We discuss using classical music for separation anxiety in the next chapter.

The most important thing about fireworks and thunderstorms is for you to remain calm. If you are on Facebook bitching about fireworks, chances are you are stressed at this time and that will affect your dog. I wish fireworks were only allowed for big corporate licensed events and not allowed for home use, as it would solve a lot of problems and be much better for animals – instead of dickheads just getting them and letting them off weeks before and weeks after Bonfire Night. But I don't see this changing any time soon.

Instead, we must stay calm, we must keep our emotions in check, and remember, if fireworks freak your dog out and you are angry, worried, anxious about your dog or the event itself, your dog will feed off your emotions. The only difference is, your dog will associate the event of fireworks going off as not only a stressful thing for them, but also for you, the person they turn to when they are afraid. And that will only make matters ten times worse.

CHILDREN DOS AND DON'TS

Now dogs and children growing up together is a magic thing; science even shows us that children who live with dogs tend to have stronger immune systems than those that don't. But dogs and children should be brought up to respect one another too. A lot of children get bitten because they try to hug the dog when it's eating, or they disturb a dog when it's sleeping. Children should always be taught not to bother a dog while it's asleep or at mealtimes. There are plenty of opportunities for a child to interact with your dog, but those times are not the right times.

Speaking of hugging dogs, many dogs don't enjoy this the way we think they do. Hugging is very much a human thing and not so much a dog thing, so don't think hugging your dog when it has snuggled up to you, or even jumped up, to be anything like when you hug your mum. Some dogs don't mind a hug, but a lot aren't keen, and just tolerate it from you. We must also remember that children will often imitate what they see us do, so it's important that if you do hug your dog, don't let your young child do it too, as the dog may not be as tolerant with your offspring as it is with you. If the child wants to and the dog is allowed on the sofa, they are welcome to sit on the sofa and invite the dog up so it can lie with them, but avoid over-the-top cuddles; it's just not worth the risk.

Another big no-no for children when it comes to dogs is that dogs are not climbing frames. We must drum this into children that dogs are not seats either, and they are not to be jumped on, poked, prodded, or pulled around by youngsters.

It goes without saying, your dog should never be left unsupervised with a small child.

You should also listen to your dog. If you see it trying to get away from a child or avoid something the child is doing, listen to the dog; don't force them into difficult situations together. Signs of stress in a dog include turning away, licking lips, and making 'whale' eyes, where a lot of the white of the eye is shown.

Now dogs should also be respectful of children. They should never jump on children, chase children, or steal from children. Your dog shouldn't use your child as a climbing frame, and it shouldn't bother your children when they are eating – the rules go both ways. If your dog does jump all over children, then make sure it's on a training lead. Make sure you are teaching the dog to be respectful of children too.

These general rules will go a long way to keeping your child safe.

Things children *can* do with dogs include:

- Throwing a ball.
- Getting involved in training (always supervised).
- Feeding the dog if it's fed from a bowl and the dog has absolutely no food aggression (once the child has put the bowl down, they should walk away and leave the dog).
- Walking the dog. Use a normal lead and give the child a longer one that's attached to the dog's harness. You have control and the child feels like they are walking the dog.

With the sudden rise in viral videos on social media of dogs and children doing supposedly cute, but actually very dangerous, things together, we are seeing more and more people not reading their dog's body language and putting themselves in situations that are dangerous. All for the sake of a viral video. Don't do this. It's not worth the risk. Teach children to respect dogs and vice versa, and life will be a joy.

TAKEAWAYS

- Behaviour problems start at home, and if problems aren't addressed, going out into the real world will be much harder
- Don't make the mistake of letting the dog repeat negative behaviour. If your dog is barking inappropriately, ask yourself what you would like them to do instead, and show them
- Form a positive association with the doorbell/front door, by rewarding your dog when it remains calm at the sound
- Visitors to your home must follow the rules when they come; this means ignoring a nervous or excitable dog completely
- Get guests to throw treats on the floor so a dog has space and is not forced to take them from a stranger

- Allow the dog to sniff visitors on its own terms, with no interaction from the guests
- Don't shut the dog away when people come to the house; focus on forming positive associations instead
- When you get a dog, start as you mean to go on. Don't reward a puppy with attention when it jumps up at you; a dog should only get fussed when it's calm
- Window barking is a common issue and is relatively easy to fix
- Use a training lead and the 'Down' command to deal with reactivity to the TV
- Implementing the three core principles should stop accidents in the house
- Marking in the house nearly always happens when the dog has no rules or boundaries in place and no routine; it's time to go back to basics
- Dogs will steal things when they haven't been taught how to behave
- The prison phase system will help you work on resource-guarding issues
- Growling is simply a way dogs communicate, but context is everything – some growling is acceptable, while some

may be an overreaction and a signal there's a need for training

- Food aggression can be a serious problem, and may need in-person training help
- Destructive behaviour is often the result of boredom; make sure your dog is exercised properly and can switch off
- Dogs are fine being on the sofa, if they wait for an invite before getting up and behave when once they are
- Try to discourage play in the house. Playing in the garden and on walks is more appropriate
- Fireworks and thunderstorms can be stressful for your dog, but don't let your own emotions affect your dog
- Effective crate training means your dog will always have a safe space to go to when it is scared of loud noises
- Consider a correctly fitted thunder jacket for dogs that find fireworks and thunder stressful
- Children should always be taught to respect a dog, and vice versa

- A dog is not a climbing frame or a seat; children should not be allowed to poke, prod or pull, and a dog should be taught not to jump on or hurt a child
- Read your dog's physical cues about what he is happy with, and don't put your child in danger

CHAPTER 7

Separation anxiety

Separation anxiety is one of the most common issues we are asked to help with at SDT, and it's really snowballed after lockdown. It's not hard to see why. Dogs that were brought into their owners' homes before the Covid pandemic had nice routines with walks one or two times a day, and they expected their owners to leave the house to go to work. Then, suddenly, during lockdown, they were given complete freedom and constant attention with their owners stuck indoors, only leaving home to walk the dog a hundred times a day. You can see how this shift was too much for dogs. Worse, when lockdown lifted and life went back to normal, people headed back to work and the constant attention and extra walks stopped. Dogs had no idea about lockdown. They didn't know there was a global pandemic. It was a massively confusing time for them. Separation anxiety, as a recognised problem, ballooned. But, of course, separation anxiety wasn't just caused by lockdown; it's always been a problem with dogs and can affect any breed of dog at any age.

So, what exactly is separation anxiety? Basically, it's when a dog can't cope with being left alone. This normally stems from lack of exercise, lack of routine, lack of structure, too much affection at the wrong time and/or not being crate trained properly so the dog is not used to switching off and spending time alone.

Separation anxiety is one of the most difficult things to fix because it requires so much self-discipline and control over your own emotions. You see, it doesn't matter how much you work on this, if you are panicking about leaving your dog because it might find it stressful, the dog doesn't know that you're panicking for that reason. The dog just knows you are panicking, and then you fuck off. This leaves the dog so much more stressed.

SO HOW DO WE BEGIN TO FIX THIS?

First up, crate train. Now, this doesn't mean you put the dog in the crate only when you are going to leave and no other time; that's a big mistake. If we do this, the crate then will represent abandonment and won't help at all. This also goes for shutting the door of the crate. If you only do that when it's time for you to leave, then the door shut part represents abandonment to your dog.

We've already discussed how important the crate is in previous chapters, but it's vitally important to help with stuff like this. So, after walks, after a rigorous play session, when you are eating, or when the kids are eating, put the dog in the crate and shut the door.

This teaches the dog that after certain activities it's time to switch off and relax, but it also teaches your dog to spend short periods of time by itself, which is key to helping separation anxiety as it introduces some moments of much-needed alone time.

Another important thing to prevent separation anxiety, which must be done before the dog goes into its crate, is exercise. Before you leave the dog, you must make sure you exercise them. After their walk, they go into the crate anyway, so this is normal behaviour that's part of the routine they expect and won't always mean you are leaving.

Proper exercise is vital. Yes, it must be done before leaving your dog in the beginning, but, as we have already discussed, it's one of the keys to a happy, healthy dog, both physically and mentally. A dog that is tired is more likely to sleep when left, especially when compared to a dog that is full of beans.

Needy dogs will often suffer from separation anxiety. So, we also need to make sure that we are not creating a needy dog by fussing them and talking to them constantly at the wrong times. If the dog is following you from room to room and always seeking attention, and in turn you reinforce this by giving the dog attention, then you are going to be making it harder when you leave.

We need to make sure that fuss, attention and stroking are on our terms, when we've asked the dog to do something, or when the dog is doing something we like. Nudging, pawing at us, whining, jumping up for attention, these all need to be redirected into an alternative better behaviour that we have asked for.

Put structure in. Don't let the dog on the sofa without invitation. Don't let the dog on your bed without invitation. Don't let the dog follow you into rooms constantly; add some down-stays or sit-stays into the mix to prevent this.

To avoid separation anxiety, we also want to desensitise the dog to all the things that represent you leaving. Things like coats, shoes and keys can often trigger your dog to get worked up as it means you are about to leave, so at random times during the day, when you are not necessarily leaving, put these things on or pick them up, then do something like make a tea or coffee, then take them off or put them down or repeat but give your dog a treat. This way, as far as the dog knows, sometimes when these things happen you leave, but sometimes when you do these things you just make a drink or, better yet, sometimes these things mean they get a reward. Actions like putting your coat on, or items like your keys or bag, are therefore no longer associated in the dog's mind with you leaving.

There are also a couple of other things that can help a dog relax:

1. **Classical music** Classical music seems to have a calming effect on dogs, so it's worth playing that from time to time throughout the day when you are at home, so that when you leave you can play it for the dog as well. Remember to not just do this when it comes time to leave, to avoid negative associations being made.
2. **Lavender** This herb also has a calming effect on dogs, so pet-friendly plug-in diffusers can be useful to have, as well as scented candles (just don't leave the candles alight when you go out!). You can also wash the dog's bedding in lavender-scented detergent to help make the bedding more relaxing, providing your dog isn't allergic to added perfumes.

IGNORE THE STOPWATCH

Now something that's important when working on separation anxiety is to not get caught up on time. For example, don't waste your time leaving the dog for one minute, then two minutes, and slowly building it up. It's so staged and unrealistic that it doesn't bear any relation to the real world. But that doesn't mean you suddenly go the other way and just leave a dog with separation anxiety for hours on end; that's not going to help either.

What you do is, if you need to go to the shop, you go to the shop. If you have to pop out for an hour, then do so, and do so without panic or stressing out. Dogs are great at working out patterns, and if you've been regimental with the time, then your dog will come to expect that. If you've been clock-watching and have got to exactly five minutes of time away from the dog but suddenly you can't get back at five minutes because we have real lives to deal with, your dog will start to panic. Try to not be so strict with the time when it comes to leaving the dog. Just make sure you are following the above advice and you will find life gets easier.

And finally, if your dog is in the crate whining when you return, it doesn't come out until it stops whining, otherwise it will do this when you leave to get you to come back.

FINAL TIPS

If you are reading this book and you have a puppy that doesn't have separation anxiety, make sure you still are following the tips above. Giving your dog proper exercise, teaching it a proper off switch via crate training, and not rewarding needy behaviour will prevent separation anxiety from happening in the first place.

And my last thought to add, guys is, *DON'T* get a second dog to help with a first dog that has separation anxiety. Remember, the dog is, more often than not, struggling with the separation from you, rather than just being on its own. But since dogs are often 'monkey see, monkey do', and will mirror the behaviours of other dogs around them (and especially if that second dog is a puppy you are bringing in), rather than cure your dog you'll more likely end up with *two* dogs with separation anxiety!

TAKEAWAYS

- Separation anxiety is a common behavioural issue and has affected more dogs since the Covid lockdown and subsequent return to normal routines
- Separation anxiety requires self-discipline and that you control your own emotions, as a dog will mimic any stress you're experiencing when you come to leave
- Correct crate training is essential to prevent and deal with separation anxiety, because your dog is learning about how to switch off

- A dog must be exercised before it is left alone and in a crate as part of your normal routine
- Needy dogs are more likely to suffer from separation anxiety
- Don't allow your dog to associate certain behaviours or items, such as putting your coat on or picking up your door keys, with leaving the house
- Classical music and using lavender scents can help relax a dog
- Don't get caught up in a rigid cycle of clock-watching
- Don't get a second dog to help your first cope with being alone; you're more likely to end up with double the problem!

CHAPTER 8

The multi-dog household

A big mistake a lot of people make is to bring a second dog into the home, when their first dog already has issues.

Common sense ought to tell us that if you are already struggling to train your first dog, training two dogs instead is going to be so much harder. Remember, dogs bond and learn quicker from their own kind than they do with and from humans. Very often what happens in this scenario is that the new dog will pick up on the bad behaviours the first dog has. Now you have two dogs with issues. Epic fail!

So, if you do want a second dog, it's always important to make sure your first dog will be a role model. Before you introduce another dog, make sure your first dog has good manners, good behaviour and understands the rules of the house inside and out. This way, life is much easier.

In this chapter we are going to discuss how to add a second dog to the home properly. But don't worry, if you've got two dogs or three dogs already, and they do have issues, we will cover that too. We'll also dig into aggression between dogs in the same house, even if it's not littermate syndrome.

In the meantime, let's start at the beginning.

LITTERMATE SYNDROME

While it's obvious that getting two dogs at the same time means you'll have double the work, it's also not advisable to get two puppies together because of a concept called littermate syndrome.

Littermate syndrome (also known as littermate aggression) is a behavioural condition that can impact the social development of dogs. Aggression, separation anxiety, fiercely protective tendencies and disruptive behaviour are all tell-tale signs of littermate syndrome. It'll usually be more apparent if you try to separate them, even briefly. Littermate syndrome can also affect puppies from different litters – for example, you get a German Shepherd at eight weeks old and then go to another breeder and get an eight-week-old Rottweiler.

Littermate syndrome occurs when two puppies of a similar age are raised in the same home and form an unhealthy reliance on one another. This bond can be seen as quite sweet at first, but the problem is that it becomes much stronger than the bond they develop with anyone else, including you.

If you choose to home two dogs from the same litter, or two dogs from different litters at the same time, there's a higher chance that they'll bond strongly with one another, making it difficult for them to form a bond with you. It's likely they'll place each other first on their priority lists, and that any attachment to you will come after that. This makes training difficult, because training relies on the dog focusing on you, understanding what you are asking it to do, and being keen to do that because they want the reward they associate with that command, including your praise when they behave appropriately.

To counteract this, it's important to make sure that if you get two pups from the same litter, or have two unrelated young puppies, you start training them individually and get them used to spending time apart from each other. This will allow you one-on-one time with them so they each bond with you. It will make training easier and teach them that it's okay to spend time apart.

Because of the known difficulties associated with littermate syndrome, it's worth mentioning that no decent breeder in their right mind would sell you two dogs from the same litter. If a breeder is pushing you to take two, or agrees to you taking two puppies without mentioning the potential for problems, you can take it as read that this isn't a reputable breeder. And if it isn't a reputable breeder, then chances are the relevant health checks haven't been done either, which may lead to heartache down the road.

I wouldn't personally consider a second dog until your first dog is at least a year old. That way you should have been able to get your first dog to a high standard of training and they will still be close enough in age that they have many years together having adventures. With this kind of age gap, littermate syndrome won't be a problem.

TRAIN DOGS INDIVIDUALLY

Although having two dogs can be very rewarding, it's important when teaching a dog something new for the first time that you do it with no distractions. Obviously, that includes another dog, as that can be a big distraction for the dog you're trying to train. I always like to spend that one-on-one time teaching each dog individual behaviours and then bring the other one into the equation once they both know it. This way you can work on them together with the best chance of success.

For example, if both dogs don't know 'Sit', work on the command on your own with just one dog and let the second chill. Then simply switch dogs, so you are training them one at a time. The added bonus is that the other dog is learning that after training comes a rest period. When both dogs know a command, you can then move on to work on it with both dogs together. If you are working on more complex behaviours, like a down-stay of some duration, and you find the addition of another dog is a distraction, don't be afraid to simplify the exercise, by reducing the time the dog holds the down position for example, to give both dogs a win.

The principle of training dogs individually also applies to lead walking, which we'll discuss in more depth later. But if they are both pulling, or both reacting, you are going to really struggle to change that behaviour, so take separate walks, fix the behaviour problems individually and then bring them together.

Now I know that's more time and more work, but this is the reality of having two or more dogs, especially if you don't train the first dog before adding another to the mix. But don't worry, it won't be forever, just until the issues are resolved.

WHEN YOUR DOGS ARE TOGETHER

Some things the dogs will need to do together, like eating and sleeping. And I need to go into these things a bit as there are common mistakes typically made in a multi-dog household within these areas.

First up, eating. A big mistake I see is that owners will always choose to feed the original dog first, every single time. Often, it's this dog that gets a treat or a walk first, whatever is happening. This can be a mistake. In a multi-dog household, you should always reward the calmest dog first. Calm dogs are not causing trouble, calm dogs listen, calm dogs are a joy to be around – remember that.

If your first dog is jumping, barking and whining, while your second dog is sitting nicely when it's dinner time, you reward that second dog. Otherwise, you are rewarding unwanted behaviour in the first dog and ignoring the good behaviour offered by the other dog. Guess what that second dog will start offering soon? That's right, the barking, jumping and whining! When dogs see that certain behaviours get them what they want, they will offer them, so make sure, whether it's one dog, two dogs, or more, you always reward the behaviours you like.

Sleeping time

In the beginning, when you are training your dog, it should be sleeping in a crate until it's issue-free. Dogs only graduate to sofas and big dog beds once they can be trusted.

So, if you have two dogs still going through training, they should both be sleeping in crates. The crates should be in the same room as each other, and they can be close to each other too. But it's important that you have one crate for each dog, and that you never put them in the same crate. You should never lock two predatory animals (which is what dogs are) in a cage together, no matter how close they are. One accident, one hiccup, and it could be disaster. It's just not worth the risk.

TOYS

Remember earlier I said that I don't like dogs having free access to toys? This is doubly important when you have several dogs. If the dogs don't see you as the one who controls the toys, very quickly they can start to think the toys belong to them and it can easily create conflict and lead to problems. Making sure the toys come out on your terms is vital to both training reinforcement and a harmonious multi-dog household.

Play fighting and playing with toys

Now a bit of play fighting is fine, and many dogs like to play rough – they will often bite, bark and jump over each other – but it's important to read rough play correctly so that you can avoid this turning into a fight.

Play must be back and forth, and not one-sided. If one dog is constantly telling off the other one, while the other is constantly turning, walking away or trying to get away then you must stop the interaction. At this point, it's no longer play and is bullying, which can lead to house fights. Even if the play is back and forth, it's still important to interrupt it frequently, every few minutes or so, and pop them both into a down-stay until calm. Then let them go back and play together. This teaches the dogs limits and reminds them that there is a human referee who is always in control.

If one dog is always rolling onto its back and being submissive you need to step in. A dog always showing its belly is something we want to avoid. If a dog does this every time it sees another dog, it's often driven by nerves. In this situation (whether it's happening between your own dogs, or if this happens with a dog outside the household) we want to advocate for our dog by stepping in between the two and getting our dog back to its feet. Dogs that roll on their backs to show submission will often end up getting bullied. It's not a positive experience for our dog and it could eventually lead to reactivity.

Remember though, guys, as fun as play is, it's also important to make sure you are working on calm activities the dogs can do together, like lead walking, obedience training, resting and just hanging out, maybe in pubs or even in the back yard. Don't forget to put the work in individually though so you can achieve this.

TREAT THEM EQUALLY BUT NOT EQUAL

What I mean by this is hold all your dogs to a high standard of behaviour and teach them what they need to do. Have a set of rules and stick to them; feed them both, walk them, love them and meet their needs. This is treating them equally, but that doesn't mean just because one dog can do something, the other one can or gets to do so too.

For example, your first dog might be older, it might be trained, it might get to be on the sofa, it might even have the freedom of the house, but your second dog, be it a rescue or a puppy, might have to have a different set of rules in the beginning. They might not be ready to have full freedom; they might not be allowed on the sofa yet. If they are young, they may need much more forced frequent nap time. This is okay.

Think of it as you might think about children, like an older sibling versus a younger sibling, for example. You love them both and they both have rules they must follow, but those rules can be different because of age and experience. Just because your teen is allowed out alone at night, it doesn't mean your ten-year-old gets the same treatment. For dog siblings, come dinner time they both get fed but the calmest one gets fed first. The mistake people make is giving a new dog or puppy the same freedoms as the existing dog when the original dog has earned that freedom previously. This is when all hell breaks loose.

GIVING AFFECTION

Affection to me is when you are stroking your dog and fussing them. This is one of the easiest things we can do with dogs, something we do way too much at times, and it's a big reason why dog fights can occur at home. When you have two dogs controlling your personal space, how and what you give as affection is so important.

But, if you call one dog over for a fuss, and then the other dog pushes its way in and you fuss that one too, one dog is being rewarded for coming to you and the other is being rewarded for being rude and pushy. It won't be long before both dogs do this, or one dog gets the hump. So, make sure both dogs are being polite before you stroke them, or if one is but the other isn't, stroke the polite one while trying to get the other one to do something you like so you can reward it with affection (e.g., use the 'Sit' command).

This applies with the sofa as well. Inviting one up doesn't mean they both jump on. They must always wait for an invitation from you, and they must settle quickly, no playing or being silly. Sofas are for rest and nothing else. Remember, it's okay to have an older dog on the sofa but not the puppy when the puppy doesn't know how to settle. The puppy will eventually get this privilege.

WHEN FIGHTING IS A PROBLEM

Now if you are strict with the rules, you should, hopefully, never have to deal with in-house dog aggression, but if you do, it's important to get a trainer to visit in person and assess the situation. This is not a problem to be ignored.

Typically, after an altercation between dogs that live together, their owners separate them without resolving the issues. So, what happens is when you bring them back together the last thing that they remember is the fight, and history repeats itself. It might also be that every time they are together again, you find yourself panicking, and the dogs feed off that and fight.

If a fight breaks out between two dogs in your home, you must separate them and do so quickly. From then on, keep one in his crate and leave the other dog out. Then swap over, putting the other dog in its crate. Whenever one is in the crate, the other is out. Implement this 'crate and rotate' system for a few days.

When a dog is out, work with that one, stripping your training back to basics and making sure your foundations are in place. Once you have worked with that dog, it returns to its crate while you work with the other dog.

They eat at the same time, but in their crates; they sleep in the same room, but in their crates; and, if there's a second person in the house, ideally the dogs are walked together by both of you.

We spoke about the importance of muzzle training earlier in the book (p.15) and muzzles can come in handy when it's time to let them out of their crates at the same time. This would be after a few days, if the animosity has settled down. But the second you start to see signs of jealous or possessive behaviours, the second you see them battling for attention or resources, that's when you get super proactive and you crate and rotate again so it doesn't escalate into a fight.

Breaking up a dog fight

A fight between dogs is one of the worst things any dog owner can experience, whether it's with another dog attacking your own dog or your own dogs getting into a fight. I hope to God you never have to experience it, but, sadly, it's something that needs to be discussed and, I'll warn you now, this is a hard read.

You might have heard bullshit like if two dogs are fighting, throw a blanket or a bucket of water over them;

you might have even heard things like stick a finger in the dog's arse, but these methods are futile and won't help if it's a serious dog fight. In fact, the quickest and most effective way to break up a dog fight is to choke the dog that's got hold of another. You can either grab the dog's collar and twist it, or, if the dog doesn't have a collar on and you have a lead, put the lead round the neck and thread it through the handle to form a makeshift slip lead that you can use to choke the dog instead. These two methods cut off the air supply, and 99 per cent of the time, a dog will let go before it passes out. But don't worry, it's not going to kill the dog, it's more like a chokehold in Mixed Martial Arts – when the person taps out, you release; think of the dog letting go as it 'tapping out'. It's because of potential situations like this that I always make sure I have a lead to hand and take a spare one on walks.

Of course, having to choke a dog is not a nice thing to have to do. Your chances of getting bitten are also extremely high when you are forced to get in the middle of a dog fight, but it's the quickest and safest way to end a fight. If you panic, scream, start hitting the dogs and trying to pull them off each other instead, that will lead to way more damage to the dogs.

But what if the attacking dog isn't your dog? This is something I get asked a lot when I do videos on the subject and the answer is simple: *it doesn't fucking matter*. I couldn't give two shits whether I know that dog or not. If it's got hold of my dog – which means I've already failed – I will do whatever it takes, no matter the cost to me, to stop it quickly. There's more on how to prevent a stranger's dog attacking your dog later in this book (p.153), because prevention is always better than the cure.

What about the wheelbarrow technique?

The wheelbarrow technique requires you to grab the dog's back legs and move around in a circle until they let go. Problem with this is, it requires two people, and most people don't know what they are doing. Relying on this method is dangerous and will only work for some dogs, and could cause way more damage than needed because some dogs will just not let go.

What about a break stick?

Break sticks are what used to be used to get a dog off a bite during dog fighting. It's an effective tool, but it has its downsides. For one, you must pry it into the dog's mouth and twist. And for another, it looks like a weapon, so if you are carrying a break stick on the streets you could find yourself in trouble with the law.

KNOW YOUR LIMITS

Before you consider adding another dog to your home, it's important to be realistic about your abilities in a multi-dog household. Making sure your first dog is properly trained will go a long way towards making things easier when you add a second dog, but don't be tempted to take on something you can't handle if the worst were to happen. Yes, it's cool to own two Rottweilers, but could you separate them if you had to, if you are being honest? Always be honest with yourself about your abilities, to avoid disaster. But I don't want to put you off! Owning two dogs is a joy. For a long time, I had three dogs. It had its ups and downs, but I don't regret a single minute of it.

Now we've covered indoors, let's have a crack at fixing those issues that dogs have outside the home.

TAKEAWAYS

- If you are already struggling to train your first dog, training two dogs is going to be so much harder
- Littermate syndrome is a behavioural condition that can impact the social development of dogs
- Dogs of a similar age that come to a home at the same time can form a bond with each other that is much stronger than the bond they develop with you
- To counteract littermate syndrome, train each dog individually and get them used to spending time apart
- Ideally don't consider a second dog until your first dog is at least a year old
- When teaching a dog something new for the first time, do it with no distractions, including any other dogs

- Dogs should never be crated together
- Regardless of which dog arrived in the house first, when they are both present, reward the one behaving the best first
- Allowing a new dog or puppy the same freedoms as the existing dog that has earned those freedoms by behaving well can cause problems
- If your dogs are fighting at home, you must call in a behaviourist to prevent the problem from escalating
- After a fight between two dogs that live together, use the 'crate and rotate' system
- If you need to break up a dog fight, the most effective way is to choke the biting dog, either by twisting its collar, or by placing a lead around its neck and tightening
- If you want to introduce another dog into your home, be realistic about your abilities

PART III
YOUR DOG OUTDOORS

CHAPTER 9

Lead walking

Lead walking is one of the most powerful exercises you can do with your dog. When it's done correctly it can reduce many of the behaviour issues you might experience, and improve other areas such as recall and attention. Correct lead walking can build confidence in a nervous dog, slow down an anxious mind and provide clarity all round. But lead walking is so much more than just attaching a lead and setting off on your way. It's a partnership, it's a bonding exercise, and it's a calming mental exercise when carried out properly. If there's one thing that nearly every dog you'll meet shares, it is that they all needed work at some point to walk nicely on a lead.

Now while I said that lead walking builds a relationship between you and your dog, you should also know that it's not a 50–50 relationship. It's more like a parent–child relationship, with the dog being the child. It's so important that you have rules in place, and that it's structured, but it must also be fun for the dog. We will cover those rules in a moment.

GIVE AND TAKE

A lot of trainers will tell you that the walk is for the dog so you should let it do whatever it wants, but this is very harmful advice. While I agree the walk is for the dog, it is also for you. It's no good if the dog is having the time of its life, but you are having your arm pulled out of its socket. It's also no good if the dog is hyper-aroused, nervous, or reacting to everything: this isn't going to be enjoyable for you or the dog.

Let me tell you, letting the dog have too much freedom and make all the choices will often lead to more problems down the line. Dogs need structure, but not in the 'you must be pack leader' way. I don't agree with that kind of crap either. That mindset leads to the type of walk where the dog is forced to walk by your side or behind you, where he must follow your every move, isn't allowed to sniff and isn't allowed in front ever. This approach is boring and unnecessary. What we're aiming for is balance, a give and take.

My idea of a good walk would be that the dog walks nicely by your side for 10 to 15 minutes, at your pace, doing as you ask, with you setting the tone. If you stop, the dog stops. If you speed up, the dog speeds up. But then, as a reward for a job well done, you ask the dog to sit, wait for eye contact and then release the dog to be in front. This is now your dog's time to explore further. If they stop, you can stop. If they stay there too long, you can usher them on but it's now the dog's time. You do this for 5 to 10 minutes or so then go back to structure, and you keep going back and forth between this. It's very important though, that whether the dog is in front of you or by your side, it's not pulling.

WHAT SIDE SHOULD THE DOG WALK ON?

Primarily when teaching a 'Heel', we put the dog on the left side. But, unless you are planning on competing with your dog, choosing which side of you your dog walks is more a personal preference. Choose whichever side you feel comfortable with. There is no scientific evidence to support the idea that dogs walk better on the left or the right. So, you do what's best for you and your dog. If you're going to use both sides at some point, I'd recommend using a different command for left and right, i.e., 'Heel' for your left side and 'Close' for your right.

WHAT TRAINING TOOLS SHOULD YOU USE?

To begin with, I like to use just a normal collar and a front clip harness with a double-ended lead. I attach one of the ends of the lead to the dog's collar and the other end to the dog's front clip on the harness. This combination allows me to control both body and head. This is a great set-up for mild pullers.

At SDT we tend not to use harnesses alone on dogs that pull. The reason for this is simple: harnesses for the best part are designed so the dog can pull comfortably. And all dogs know how to pull! General excitement, and the fact they have four legs while we only have two, means they often move faster than us. A harness makes pulling much easier and gives more of the control to the dog. You can of course use a harness to teach a dog to walk nicely, but it's going to take so much longer than necessary. Instead, using a harness with a collar means you can have full control and steer the dog where you want them. It also means that if the dog is really pulling, the combination of the two takes a lot of pressure off the throat, so no choking. This harness-and-collar combo can be used right from the first walk.

For big pullers I would maybe consider something like a Halti or Dogmatic. These are headcollars that give you much more control. It's important if you use a Halti though that you take the time to condition your dog to it, so he's comfortable wearing one. To condition your dog to wearing a Halti, go back to p.15 and use the instructions for muzzle conditioning. A Halti can be used once a dog reaches six months of age.

WHAT IS A HALTI?

The Halti headcollar was invented over thirty years ago and is a bit like a halter worn by horses. Also known as a gentle leader or head halter, the Halti basically goes over the dog's head with the bigger loop going around the dog's neck and the smaller loop going over the dog's muzzle. A correctly worn Halti should provide enough space to allow one finger to slide under the cheek strap, meaning it won't interfere with panting, eating or drinking.

Slip leads

Slip leads are another tool we use a lot as they're great for controlling the dog and for teaching pressure. This is because, if a slip lead is fitted correctly, it sits snugly right at the top of a dog's neck and distributes any pressure equally. This is not like a normal collar which puts all the pressure at the base of the throat. This allows for better communication with your dog. However, the slip lead itself doesn't stop the dog pulling and nor will any tool. The tool is an aid; you have to teach the dog what it means. No matter what tool you use, it's important that it's used correctly.

How To Train Your Dog

'Password: SDTBook'

HOW TO BEGIN LEAD WALKING

The first thing to remember is that your dog should *always* be calm at the start of the walk. Don't say, 'Do you want to go walkies?' Of course the dog wants to go for a walk! All you're doing by saying this is creating a precursor for excitement and encouraging your dog to go mental. Excitement will make pulling more likely. Think back to our threshold advice on p.59.

You also want to make sure the dog doesn't go mental simply at the sight of the lead. To avoid this, you want to pick up the lead you use for walking regularly throughout the day and move it. Even when you're not going on a walk. You might get some initial excitement as the dog thinks the lead always means walk, but quickly the dog will realise you picking up the lead is just that. The association between you picking up a lead and then going for a walk will be broken.

When it is time for the walk, call your dog to you and attach the lead. If the dog goes crazy, sit down for a minute and wait for the dog to calm down. When the dog is calm you want to go to the door. But before you open the front door, you want to make sure that the dog is behind you and not in front of you, you should be between the dog and the door, and the dog should be in a sit. Next, open the door. If the dog comes out of the sit, shut the door and reset. Rinse and repeat until you can get the door open and the dog is sitting nicely behind you. When you have eye contact, lead the dog through the front door or say 'Heel' if your dog knows that command (learn how to teach 'Heel' on p.58); don't say 'Okay', 'Break' or 'Go on then'. These are often words that mean the dog can go run and play and is essentially free, so this will undo what we want. We want a calm dog ahead of the walk. As soon as you are outside, put the dog back into a sit (remember sit means sit) and shut the front door.

If you follow the above instructions, you're starting the walk the right way straight away and you will see a massive difference. If you don't start in the right way, like most people, you'll fail the walk before it's even begun. Don't worry if following the advice at the start of the walk takes a long time. This approach is a mental exercise, which is draining, but what takes a long time today will get shorter each day and easier each day *if* you are consistent. Then you'll have years of calm walks ahead of you both.

PRO TIPS

I recommend you practise auto stops, or what we at SDT call 'applying the brakes'. To do this, every few minutes or so and for no reason, gently pull up on the lead and come to a stop and pop the dog in a sit. We want the dog to learn that any time we stop, whether it's because we have to or just because, the dog is to go into a sit. This will help massively if you have a reactive dog on the lead (more information on that in Chapter 11). Just bear in mind some dogs, like sighthounds, have trouble sitting comfortably because of their anatomy, while older dogs may be arthritic. If this is the case for your dog, try asking for a 'Stop' position instead. If your dog is struggling to sit and you don't know why, a visit to the vet might be in order.

Another thing to make sure we are doing is holding the lead, short but relaxed, by our side. The lead should have just enough slack in it so that when our dog is by our side there is no tension, but as soon as the dog goes rogue and starts to go in front, we feel that tension and we gently pull up. Pulling up slows the dog down. Don't pull back though, as pulling back often creates an opposition reflex and makes a dog pull more.

USING A BACKPACK

Finally, if the dog is a big puller and very high energy, a specially designed weighted dog backpack can help massively. Backpacks are suitable for adult dogs (not puppies) who have no health or joint problems. The idea behind the backpack is that it gives the dog a job to do and something to focus on. Dogs are notoriously rubbish at multi-tasking, so often when they are carrying something they can focus on that and they then become calmer, slower and more attentive.

Now, you might say, 'But my dog's breed wasn't designed to carry things.' You'd be surprised though how many dogs respond to a variety of jobs. Think of a Labrador for example; this is a versatile breed that's mastered everything from search and rescue to guiding the blind. Lots of dogs will benefit from carrying a weighted backpack.

Typically, when choosing a backpack, you don't need to go heavier than 10 per cent of the dog's body weight. For example, for a 30kg dog a good weight would be 1.5kg either side of the backpack (meaning 3kg total). Backpacks are for lead walking, and you should never ask your dog to carry more than 10 per cent of its body weight. A dog shouldn't be wearing a backpack when they are running, chasing, or playing as these are individual activities separate from the 'job' of wearing a backpack. The backpacks we use are on our website, and the weights we recommend are bags of sand, weighed on your kitchen scales and then put into a sandwich bag and wrapped up in duct tape. If the weight is right, you should see a slower, calmer dog.

TAKEAWAYS

- Approach lead walking as a partnership, but it's not a 50–50 relationship
- When done correctly it can reduce many of the behaviour issues you might already experience
- You should aim for a bit of give and take on the perfect walk; sometimes you choose what will happen, other times your dog might set the pace
- Choose which side of you your dog walks on, based on your own preference
- A normal collar and a front clip harness with a double-ended lead is perfect to start lead walking
- A Halti or Dogmatic headcollar can help with pulling – but you must condition your dog to a headcollar first
- A slip lead can be a useful tool if used correctly

- Break the association between you reaching for the lead and a walk being on the cards by randomly picking up your dog's lead throughout the day
- Start your walk in a calm manner. It may take time to teach this at first, but it will be worth it for years to come
- Teaching your dog auto stops and sits (or a suitable alternative) during the walk will help you if problems arise
- Dogs that struggle to walk calmly on a lead will benefit from wearing a weighted backpack
- A weighted backpack should never be heavier than 10 per cent of the dog's total body weight

CHAPTER 10

Socialisation

Socialisation means teaching your dog how to be comfortable in the real world, which is full of unfamiliar smells, sights and sounds. These include those that come from other people, dogs and animals, as well as vehicles, environments and objects. Life is incredibly varied; outside your home your dogs may encounter small children on scooters one minute and a police car whizzing past with its siren blaring the next. When you're out on a longer walk, you may need to safely pass horses, wild or farm animals, runners and cyclists. Some of these things may happen quickly. It's incredibly important to socialise your dog and build his confidence around these things, so that he doesn't become fearful and potentially reactive. The aim is to have a calm and confident dog that can take the unexpected in their stride and still respond to your commands despite any distractions.

For a full list of places, people, situations and things you should get your dog used to, turn to the checklist on p.146.

It's also worth mentioning that the guidelines for socialisation work for any new dog, whatever his age, and any dog that is new to socialisation.

WHAT SOCIALISATION IS NOT

Lots of people make the mistake of thinking that socialising a puppy or new dog just means going to the park and letting the dog off to run about like crazy with every single dog it meets there. But there's so much more to it than that, and in fact allowing your dog to do what he wants without giving him any guidance is just about the worst way to approach socialisation.

It's also incredibly boring for your dog to return to the same place over and over, rather than adding to his experience of a variety of places. If you just repeat the same walk every day, your dog will be overwhelmed when you need to go elsewhere. Instead, you need to approach this key part of your dog's training seriously. I like to break it down into three key areas: the environment, animals and humans.

Incidentally, when you are out socialising your dog, you should continue with all your training. This teaches your dog to pay attention to you and listen to your commands everywhere it goes. You'll create a dog that's bombproof.

ENVIRONMENT

Proper environmental exposure is about taking your dog to many different places to let them see, feel and experience as many different sights, sounds and smells as possible. Think about the variety of terrains, from beach to park to woods to open fields, you can explore. You might be walking on grass, sand, mud, gravel or tarmac.

Then consider all the different weather conditions and temperatures that you could be out in, from sun and wind to rain to ice and snow. Environmental socialisation also includes areas with lots of people that you might want to take your dog along to, including pubs, shops, fetes and fairs, town centres, on public transport, as well as the homes of friends and relatives.

With regard to the places you take your dog, bear in mind the characteristics of the type or breed of dog you have. A terrier will need somewhere to explore, while a Chihuahua isn't built for mountain hikes! While you should introduce your dog to all types of environments so that they have a positive experience of, say, both town and country, choose your regular walks in places that they will be able to thoroughly enjoy.

ANIMALS

This isn't about making sure your dog has the most friends! It's really about teaching your dog how to behave around other animals, and while that does include other dogs, it also means animals like sheep, cows and horses you might see on your walks, the cats and small furries that could be in your own home or houses you visit, the birds and squirrels in the park, and even the wildlife in your garden like night-time visitors such as foxes and hedgehogs. By all means, carefully introduce your dog to the other dogs in the neighbourhood when you're at the local park, but just don't think socialising your dog starts and ends there.

It's also worth remembering that rather than wanting

a dog that approaches every animal it sees, eagerly expecting it to play with them, what you're really aiming for is a pooch that is happy to ignore other animals. I call it being 'socially ignorant'. You and your family should be your dog's priority, and their bond lies with you, not every other dog in the park. A dog that isn't overexcited to meet other animals is a dog that remains calm when it does. And a calm dog is a happy and safe dog.

When your dog first meets other animals, including new dogs, keep him on a lead and practise the art of attention. You should aim to break your dog's focus from the new, potentially exciting animal and always bring it back to you. Use a toy or a treat to get your dog's attention, practise those basic commands, and mark and reward your dog when it listens to you. Teach your dog that in all situations, the best, most rewarding thing is to focus on you.

If you're happy for your dog to meet another dog when they are both off lead, I recommend using the three-second rule. Allow the dogs three seconds to sniff each other, and then call yours back to you. If they don't come back, use the lead to ensure they do. Mark and reward when they do come back. Keeping it short and sweet prevents the dogs from getting overexcited and the situation from spiralling. You can reintroduce the two dogs after a few minutes.

And once you're confident your dog's loyalties lie with you, you can then select the dogs it meets and plays with regularly. And you'll be secure in the knowledge that when it's time to stop playing, your dog will listen to you. If you're having trouble finding suitable dog playmates, because no one in your social circle has a dog, consider a training club that offers controlled socialising sessions.

PEOPLE

This is another case of quality over quantity. Don't let all and sundry rush up to your dog and get him all excited, teaching him bad habits and potentially scaring the living daylights out of him. You decide who talks to your dog and you make the rules. While some people won't mind a puppy leaping up at them, many will, and it won't be so adorable once the dog is fully grown. You want to aim for a nice, calm meet-and-greet so you can teach expected behaviour – strangers with excited voices are out! Instead, if you're happy for your dog to meet someone, ensure the pup is sitting well and is calm, and then allow the hello. Mark and reward the good behaviour.

Also check your dog's reaction when strangers approach and be his advocate. Look for signs that he may be uncomfortable, and instead of forcing him to endure something he doesn't want to do, get him out of the situation before he forms what could become a negative association. Take the lead. Literally and figuratively! If your dog is turning or backing away, looking nervous by licking his lips or showing a lot of his eye whites (called 'whale eye') then that's a dog politely making his excuses.

COMMON MISTAKES

One of the main problems I see when people hit a bump in the road socialising a puppy or new dog is the desire to mollycoddle or baby them. If your dog is frightened of a new thing they haven't experienced before, be it a recycling bag left on the pavement or a puddle in a field, lead by example and don't panic. Stroking or fussing them may act to reward their behaviour, making them think being frightened is the response you want to see. Shorten up your lead and walk on with confidence. Be firm and confident. Your dog will follow.

Never let your dog go 'free range' and greet every dog it sees without any guidance from you. They may come across a dog that isn't friendly, and a negative experience will stay with them and possibly lead to fear and reactivity in the future. They may also learn that it's more fun to hang out with all the other dogs that don't listen to their owners than it is to come back to you and go home for nap time. Instead, introduce your dog to other dogs that you know well, whose owners you are likely to see because they are friends and family. Choose dogs that behave well and owners that have control of their dogs.

Don't fall into the trap of treating your dog like a mini human and thinking it needs what you do. This is called anthropomorphism, and it is when you think about animals as if they were human. You'll be looking for human-like qualities in your pets and believe that your dog is experiencing emotions like a human would. But this isn't the case! So, when it comes to socialising your pet, he doesn't need a group of mates to meet down the park, like you might need a group of mates to meet down the pub, and he doesn't understand when you say, 'There there, it's okay, the carrier bag flapping in the bush isn't going to hurt you.'

Avoid going to the same place and doing the same thing day in, day out with your dog. It's dull as ditchwater for one, but it's also not preparing your pup for anything else. A dog that's overwhelmed by new places or a sudden change of routine will struggle to pay attention to you. Mix it up; visit some unusual places; use the checklist (p.146) to make it fun.

Another thing to remember is that an owner's state of mind can impact how a dog behaves. While this is a hard one to get over, if you're finding something difficult when socialising your dog, it's likely he can sense that too. Unfortunately, this can reinforce negative associations, so you must focus on being your most confident you in these situations. Do it for your dog.

'IT'S OKAY, THEY'RE FRIENDLY!'

If there's one type of owner you *don't* want to be, it's the jerk whose dog is running up to others while they fail to call it back. Odds on, these people will be miles away from their dog, shouting over that it's 'okay' and that the dog heading towards you at top speed is 'friendly'. You're unlikely to hear them call 'Come', because they know they have no recall over their pet whatsoever. Their dog is rude and out of control. You want to give them a wide berth!

If you do see a dog belting over, put yours behind you and shield them with your body. Be firm with the incoming dog, stamp your foot or shout at it (expletives allowed). If necessary, feel free to shoo or push the other dog away. You are looking out for your dog; your job is to earn their trust by protecting them.

CHALK IT UP TO EXPERIENCE

No one gets it right all day every day. You will make mistakes and have days that could have gone better. Life isn't predictable and neither is your dog. You can't avoid difficult situations, but you can try and handle them in the best way. If you've had a disappointing socialisation experience, ask yourself what went wrong and what you can do better the next time. It's how you learn. There will be good days too.

SOCIALISATION CHECKLIST

If you have read my first book you may already be familiar with some of the items on this chart, although I've added even more. The chart contains a whole load of places and situations you should help your dog feel comfortable with and around.

People	Other animals	Sights and sounds
Wearing backpacks	Puppies	Sirens
Dancing	Older dogs	Fireworks
Running	Male adult dogs	Car horns
Riding a bike	Female adult dogs	Motorbikes
Different ethnicities	Different breeds, types and sizes of dog	Thunderstorms
Men with beards	Dogs with different temperaments	Wheelchairs
Men with deep voices	Dogs with black fur and fur that covers their face	TVs
Tall people	Flat-faced dogs	Cars
Wearing hats	Kittens	Trucks
Wearing sunglasses	Cats	Buses
Toddlers	Horses	Trains
Infants	Small furry pets	Doorbells
Teenagers	Farm animals including chickens, pigs, sheep and cows in fields	Skateboards
Elderly	Squirrels	Scooters
Children playing		Prams
Clowns		Aeroplanes
Walking with canes or other mobility aids		Vacuum cleaners
Street performers		Hairdryers
		Alarms

Groups of people Those with walking sticks or poles 'Lollipop' men/women School gate crowds	Rabbits Birds Forest animals where possible Ducks, swans, geese	Washing machines Large crowds of people Traffic lights & zebra crossings Team sports/playing field cheering Loudspeakers Bands
Being handled Being weighed Checking the ears Opening the eyelids Handling and trimming nails Examining and brushing the teeth Taking tablets Using a grooming brush Touching tail Touching belly Squeezing paws Bending towards the pup Grabbing the collar Hugging your pup Holding the dog/cradling him in arms Picking up your dog to place in the car, etc.	**Places** Parks Lakes Forests/woods Seaside/beach Rivers Shopping areas Boarding kennels Day care Pet shop Vet Groomer Night trips Pubs and cafes Street fairs & community events Places a dog might swim Dog friendly: Classes Events Restaurants Races Dog shows	**Objects and terrains** Muzzles Pots and pans Brooms Wheelbarrows Umbrellas Balloons Bags blowing in the wind Bins & recycling bags/boxes Road signs Benches Escalators Lifts Tiled floors Wooden floors Carpet Stairs Wet grass Sand Mud Puddles Gravel Gates and stiles Bridges Statues Scarecrows Boats/kayaks/paddleboards Doggy buoyancy aids

TAKEAWAYS

- Life is incredibly varied outside your home; you need to socialise your dog so he is ready to be confident in the real world
- Correctly socialising your dog will prevent it from becoming fearful and potentially reactive
- There's so much more to socialising than taking your dog to a park and letting it run around with every other dog there
- At SDT we break socialising down into three key areas: environment, animal and human
- Environmental exposure means taking your dog to different places to let them see, feel and experience as many different sights, sounds and smells as you can
- Socialising your dog around other animals requires you to teach him how to behave around all sorts of other animals, small and large, feathered and furry (and even scaly!)
- You should aim to break your dog's focus from the new, potentially exciting animal, and always bring it back to you
- Use the three-second rule for new dog meets
- Don't let all and sundry rush up to your pup; aim for calm and controlled meet-and-greets with people

- Don't mollycoddle your dog if it is afraid of something – you could reinforce his fear
- Don't let your dog go 'free range' and greet every dog he sees without any guidance from you
- Avoid anthropomorphising your dog
- A dog that's overwhelmed by new places will struggle to pay attention to you
- An owner's state of mind can impact how a dog behaves; remain calm and confident in new situations
- Avoid the jerk whose dog is running up to others while they fail to call it back
- If an off-lead dog charges you, advocate for your dog and stand between them, forcing the other dog to back off
- Use any bad days as an opportunity to learn

CHAPTER 11

Reactivity

There are a multitude of different reasons why your dog might be reactive outside the home, although the resulting behaviour could look the same. These reasons include:

- Fear
- Anxiety
- Frustration
- Excitement
- Pain
- Illness

Dogs can be reactive to a singular thing, such as other dogs, particular types of people, fireworks, cars, bikes, horses, or something completely random like dustbin lids. A dog might also be reactive to a combination of things. Either way, it's important for us to understand exactly what it is that triggers reactivity in our dogs to be able to help them. You can do this by observing exactly what happens or what your dog sees before the reactive behaviour kicks in.

You can also observe your dog's body language to work out what they are experiencing. A fearful dog may freeze and tuck its tail under its body, while an aggressive dog will growl, stare and wag its tail (it's a common misconception that a dog only wags its tail to show it is friendly). Yawning, licking lips, turning the head away and panting can all be signs that your dog is unhappy in its current situation – and wants to get away.

As a self-preservation instinct, dogs will often cover up pain very well. A dog in pain may, however, show similar behaviour to a dog that is frightened or stressed by shaking, panting and keeping its ears flattened. If your dog is excessively licking or scratching a specific area of its body, or is suddenly reluctant to walk, play or eat, this could indicate pain.

As we've mentioned in this book already, muzzle training when you're dealing with a reactive dog is essential. It's also important to have a full vet check of any dog that is showing reactive behaviour to rule out any physical causes.

CAN'T SPOT A REACTIVITY PATTERN?

If you're struggling to spot a pattern to your dog's behaviour, consider the journalling we discussed in Chapter 4. This should help you pinpoint what and when your dog is most reactive and make you more self-aware too.

WHAT IS REACTIVITY?

Reactivity is a blanket term and one that is quite often misunderstood. Reactivity can cover lots of behaviours, from whining, barking and lunging to a full-blown attack and bite on someone or something. Any excessive barking that you haven't asked for, be it at home, in the garden or out and about, is reactive and anxious behaviour and is a sign your dog is stressed.

People assume that a reactive dog is an aggressive dog but that's not always the case. Even 'friendly' dogs can be reactive. For example, if your dog charges over to someone and is barking, even if it's not going to bite them this is still classed as reactive behaviour and can be dangerous. If your dog is small and might not seem to pose a threat to a much larger dog it approaches in this way, since other dogs don't care about size it is still reactive behaviour and can still be dangerous for all those involved. Even barking at passers-by from your car is reactive behaviour.

In many cases reactivity can lead to full-blown aggression. I define an aggressive dog as one that will physically do harm to another dog, another animal or a person. If your dog is aggressive and a bite risk, make sure it is muzzled as a safety precaution and don't wait another minute to call in a trainer. Dogs that have bitten will likely bite again because they have learnt it achieves the result they want (usually that the thing/person the dog is reacting to moves away). Wearing a muzzle to avoid any further bites can be the difference between your dog remaining with you or being seized and put to sleep.

WHAT CAUSES REACTIVITY?

Common causes of reactivity are a lack of socialisation, poor genetics and breeding, previous bad experiences, a lack of direction and even poor handling, particularly if a dog is given too much freedom too soon.

When puppies are reared in very low-welfare environments, the breeding bitch has often never experienced kind handling or interaction with humans. The mother is therefore fearful of humans and teaches her pups this. Mass-produced puppies are also bred without relevant health checks and care, and any aggressive genes or physical defects that can cause pain (and therefore reactivity) quickly enter the gene pool. Taking a puppy away from its mother too soon, usually before a pup is eight weeks old (another trick of the low-welfare breeder), can also cause problems.

A lack of well-thought-out socialisation at an early age can also mean a dog comes to fear many situations we would consider part of everyday life simply because they haven't got enough experience. Likewise, if a dog is allowed to do as it pleases when it is young, it may have an unpleasant experience – such as when it runs up to a dog that does not want to be approached and is bitten. A negative experience like this can happen to any dog at any time, of course. For example, a bike may knock into a well-behaved dog, an unmonitored child might hurt a dog accidentally through rough handling, or an unexpectedly loud traffic noise could cause a dog to startle.

We can also trigger a reaction in our dogs and make them reactive. For example, if your dog gets attacked by a German Shepherd, you worry this is going to affect your dog. The next time you are out and see a German Shepherd, you panic and BOOM, your dog reacts. You think it's because of what happened to your dog, but it could be the dog is feeding from your reaction because you are holding on to your feelings about what happened. And while there is such a thing as a 'single learning experience', where something bad happens to your dog one time and this changes your dog's personality for the worse, a lot of the time it's *our* fears and worries that drive a reaction from your dog.

Another example of a dog mimicking your reactions is if you are worried your dog might react. Imagine, for example, that a person is approaching you on a bicycle, and as you are preparing for it to happen, you tense up. The dog senses how you feel and then reacts because of this. Now your dog learns what made you tense up and makes a negative association to it. Even our own fears can rub off on our dogs. Fear of bangs, fear of walking alone, fear of strange dogs or people, all these things can be picked up by our dogs. So, it's super important, if we really want to help a dog, to make sure we work on ourselves as well.

Using the wrong training tools, or not knowing how to use them properly, can also cause reactivity or make reactive behaviour worse. An example of this could be using Halti but not conditioning your dog to it adequately first; or holding your lead with too much tension. Both these problems could cause your dog to panic.

Another reason I see dogs becoming reactive is a lack of exercise. People don't walk their dogs enough, or experience problems and so stop walking their dog altogether. But that pent-up energy has to go somewhere and, if other forms of stimulation such as brain games aren't offered, this can come out as reactivity.

If your dog is finding walking stressful, rather than giving up on walking altogether look to take three very short walks, where exposure will be minimal, rather than two long walks, which may be overwhelming. Or if your dog is struggling in busy areas, you could benefit in the beginning from either shortening the walk a bit or changing the time of day so it's quieter.

Earlier I mentioned frustration as a reason for reactivity. While this can stem from lack of exercise, it can also be caused by poor socialising. And when I say poor socialising, what I mean is that because you've let your dog say hello to as many dogs and people as possible, it's now become an expectation. Then, when the dog can't say hello for whatever reason – maybe the other dog or person it wants to greet isn't keen, maybe you just don't have time that day – it gets frustrated and reacts.

Be aware that there are two distinct 'fear imprint' stages for a dog. The first is around eight to twelve weeks, and the second occurs from six months up to about fourteen months. It's worth knowing about these time frames, and, if problems occur, don't panic, simply go back to basics and practise things your dog can excel at to improve his confidence.

PREVENTION AND CURE

There are so many reasons why your dog might be reactive, but regardless of where the reactivity is coming from, we are going to go through some basics that can help any dog with such behaviour. These techniques can also be used with a dog that's not reactive as a way of preventing reactivity from happening. Much of the information deals with seeing another dog as a trigger, but the methods work just as well with anything that your dog reacts to, including cars and bikes. Along with what you've learnt so far from this book, learning these general approaches will be a game-changer.

The first thing we are going to focus on is lead reactivity. The reason for this is simple. Your dog should not be off the lead if it's reactive, especially if it's going to go charging over to someone or something. Often when we fix the lead reactivity part, the rest will follow.

It's also important to note that if you've mastered my three core principles from Chapter 3, if you have addressed the issues in the house, and if you are consistent in all other areas, major problems like reactivity are much easier to address and resolve themselves much quicker. You have to look at dealing with reactivity as you would building a house. When it comes to building a house, you don't start with the roof as there would be no foundations to lay it on and it would just collapse. Well, reactivity is the roof, and to really fix it we must knuckle down on our foundations.

So, as I said, if we want to resolve reactivity, first we want to nail the lead walking, then we want to make sure we are relaxed and we want to give the dog something to focus on. Using backpacks can be a great tool if you have a reactive dog, because it can slow the dog down and give it a job, which helps the dog focus on the task at hand instead of the environment around it (and the reactivity triggers within it).

SNIFF YOUR WAY TO SUCCESS

Reactive dogs are a bit like snipers: they are just using their eyes and looking around, waiting for a stimulus to explode at. More often than not, reactive dogs are visually oriented, and they very rarely use their nose. So, we want to get that nose engaged instead. Remember, a dog takes in information through their nose; it's such a powerful thing, and when they are using it they are often curious, focused. For a dog, sniffing is mentally enriching and helps calm them down. We want to encourage the use of the nose more to help with reactivity.

How do we do this exactly? The answer might surprise you...because we use the eyes! It's time to practise the art of attention. With reactive dogs I like to use a clicker. We need to make sure the dog understands the clicker first, but the clicker is how we will get that nose engaged. It's simple really – you use the clicker as soon as your dog sees a trigger (something it's likely to react to). But the real secret is to click the clicker *before* your dog has a chance to react. Your dog will hear the clicker and focus on you because, through your earlier training, your dog has already associated that clicker sound with the fact a treat is coming (most likely food!).

Next, we move backwards with a handful of treats, for a few steps, luring the dog towards us, thus creating some space between your dog and the trigger, and then we drop the treats on the floor. Now the reason we put the treats on the floor is because it keeps the eyes down, away from the trigger, engages the nose and drags out the reward. It becomes more rewarding and more enriching for the dog. But don't worry, this won't encourage your dog to search for food on the floor going forward; the dog knows the food comes from you.

So, it's: click, step back a few steps for space, put treats down on the floor.

Now we repeat the above every time we see a trigger. What will start to happen is your dog will begin to look at a trigger and then look back at you for the expected reward. This also give us an opportunity to click and reward. We are creating a pattern of behaviour; the dog looks at a trigger (another dog, for example), then looks at us and gets a reward.

This changes the dog's emotional response to how they perceive the trigger, so instead of it creating a stress response in our dog that leads to him reacting, it's now creating a feel-good response because the trigger now equals treat.

This technique is known as counter conditioning. Here is some need-to-know information for this method:

1. If your dog doesn't break focus from the trigger when you click, stop clicking. In this situation, the fixation is too great, and you need to manually break the fixation instead. To do this, I like to pull up on the lead, turn into the dog and walk off, creating a bit more space. Then I'll start again.

2. Space is key in this method, so practising this in fields or other places where you will see dogs – or can set up another trigger – but still have lots of room to work with will help massively. The more space, the easier it is for the dog to cope.

3. If your dog doesn't take food when it's outside the home, start to hand feed at home. This will help massively with your dog accepting food from your hand when out and about. Still drop the food as outlined above, even if the dog doesn't take it. Often the food will still bring the eye line down and activate the nose.

THE 'SNIFF' COMMAND

I also like to teach reactive dogs the 'Sniff' command. It can then be used to prompt sniffing, which helps to calm the dog when you find yourself in a challenging situation. To teach this command, just say 'Sniff' and throw a treat on the grass or ground. Practise this action often and at random times when there is nothing going on for best results. If you see a trigger and your dog knows the 'Sniff' command, even if the treats are already on the floor and your dog is ignoring them you can use the command to get them to sniff and possibly take the food on the floor, breaking their focus and helping them to relax.

If your dog has toy drive, you can also use toys to help your training, especially if your dog likes things like tug. Use the marker 'Yes' when your dog sees a trigger, step back and engage in a game of tug. While this won't engage the nose, it does engage in play, which also can help a dog relax.

And if your dog likes both, why not mix it up and use a combination of the above?

TOP SPOTS TO PRACTISE

Some good places to take a dog-reactive dog so you can practise these techniques include somewhere like a pet-shop car park, or the car parks of woods and dog parks. Here you'll see plenty of dogs and people coming and going but you'll also have plenty of space to play with. These methods also work in a proactive way and going places like this to work on our dog's behaviour will reduce the chances of it becoming reactive to other dogs too.

If you want to encourage more sniffing generally to help you with counter conditioning, try woodland walks and country parks. A good 'sniff walk', where the dog gets to use his nose for almost the entirety of the walk, is always a good idea. As long as your dog isn't dragging you along, a sniff walk is enriching, providing confidence and mental stimulation, plus it tires your dog out. This can help massively with reactive dogs.

As you work with counter conditioning, you might wonder how to measure your progress. A good indicator that you're successfully using the method is if you notice that when you approach a known trigger for your dog (e.g., another dog, a car, a person on a bike), instead of focusing on the trigger your dog looks to you, expecting a reward. When this happens, you know you're on the right track. When this is happening consistently you can begin to draw out the rewards, be slower to reward and reward intermittently or randomly. You can also use praise rather than food rewards. Now you can focus on enjoying the process, happy that you've made progress:

an emotion that will rub off on your dog too, with less stressful walks becoming the norm.

However, there's no defined timeline for working with reactivity. For some dogs a change in tools or mindset might bring an immediate improvement. But how quickly reactivity improves will depend on everything from how deep-rooted the problem is and how hard you work, to how consistent you are, your own confidence and the opportunities you have for exposure to triggers.

IT'S NOT YOU, IT'S ME

The last thing I want to talk about is mindset. In Chapter 4 we discussed how important it is that we as dog owners have the right mindset. To help your dog you must get over any worries you have about what others might be thinking about you. This fear of judgement will often hold us back and in turn hinder our dog's progress. Remember, you don't owe anyone an explanation about your dog's behaviour; you don't have to tell anyone why you are doing what you are doing or why your dog might be in a muzzle. You don't owe anyone anything.

Equally, we must also ensure our dog has the right mindset. Taking a dog out that's already overexcited sets them up to fail. Think back to our threshold training, to our lead walking. Calm minds before we've even left the house are what we want. Slow down, take your time and breathe, guys.

Remember, your reactive dog isn't giving you a hard time. He's *having* a hard time and he needs you to work with him to overcome this problem. Your dog needs to see you as his rock, that can't be moved or broken, his rock that is calm, confident, consistent and decisive.

As a final word on reactivity, if your dog is a bite risk, muzzle train him for his own safety, and the safety of others.

TAKEAWAYS

- There are many different reasons why your dog might be reactive, although the resulting behaviour may look the same
- Always have a full vet check of any dog that is showing reactive behaviour to rule out any physical problems
- Even 'friendly' dogs can be reactive
- Common causes of reactivity are a lack of socialisation, poor genetics and breeding, previous bad experiences, a lack of direction and poor handling
- Our fears and worries can drive a reaction from our dog, particularly if we panic and tense up when we see a suspected trigger
- The techniques we teach at SDT apply to all triggers – and can also work proactively to prevent your dog from developing reactive behaviour

- Always work on lead reactivity first, as you may find this helps with other reactivity problems
- If you have mastered the basics and are practising the three core principles, dealing with reactivity will be far simpler
- A reactive dog should not be off the lead and able to rush up to another dog, animal or person
- Backpacks are a great tool for reactive dogs, giving them a job to focus on instead of focusing on a trigger
- Reactive dogs are often visually oriented, but we want to encourage the use of the nose to help with reactivity
- Using clicker training is the best way to counter condition your dog to look at you rather than the trigger – and to associate the trigger with a positive reward
- The 'Sniff' command is an essential command to help a reactive dog break focus from a trigger
- Practise counter conditioning in areas where you will likely see triggers but still have space to work in, like the car parks at popular dog-walking spots
- Journalling can help you spot a pattern to your dog's reactivity

- Both you and your dog must be calm before you leave for a walk, as having the right mindset is essential
- If your dog is a bite risk, muzzle train him and always muzzle when necessary

CHAPTER 12

Recall

Recall is one of the most important commands you will ever teach your dog. It's non-negotiable and can be the difference between life or death. Even if you never let your dog off the lead, you still need a reliable recall because real life never stops, and you don't want to wait until an emergency arises to have to successfully recall your dog.

Recall for the best part is a free behaviour. If you have taught your foundations properly, if you have been consistent with your training and relationship building, if you've met the needs of the dog, then the dog's recall should start to become second nature, because it wants to be with you.

TOO SOON

A big mistake we make when it comes to recall, and a reason why so many people struggle with it, is because they let the dog off the lead too soon and bad behaviours quickly imprint. If your dog runs over to the other side of the field or to a distraction such as another dog and you don't and can't stop it, in that moment that dog learns two things: first, I can have fun without you; and, second,

I don't have to listen. Guess what happens thereafter? Your recall goes right out the window.

Behaviour is based on the simple logic that dogs will always do what they find most rewarding, and if they can, they will. This is also why we are selective in the beginning with who we let our dogs play with and who we let them say hello to. We don't want the dog thinking that it can go and say hello to every person and every dog because, ultimately, this will work against us when doing recall training.

Another big mistake people make is letting dogs off the lead before they have hit adolescence. Many times, puppies can have a decent recall, but as soon as that six- to eight-month mark hits, suddenly they stop listening; they get bolder and braver and more defiant. People are often lured into a false sense of security before this teenage phase, and they think recall is done and dusted.

NO RECALL, NO CONTROL

Do you know who are the worst kind of dog owners? Those people who shout, 'It's okay, he's friendly!' as their dog runs over to something or someone because they can't stop it. Don't be that person! The only reason anyone is shouting that is because they have no recall, and they know shouting 'Come' won't work.

If your dog has no recall and you let the dog off the lead, you have no control over it. No control means your dog is out of control. Out-of-control dogs are a danger to themselves, even if they are friendly. They can run over to the wrong person, wrong dog, wrong animal, wrong distraction and into the wrong place (like a road) and disaster can ensue. Nearly every dog-on-dog attack is caused by a dog running over to the wrong dog – and then disaster strikes.

It's also a legal thing. In the eyes of the law, your dog must always be under control, and if it's not, because you let it off the lead when it's not ready, you are breaking the law. In the UK, if you are convicted of having a dog that is dangerously out of control, you can get an unlimited fine or be sent to prison for up to six months, or both. You may also not be allowed to own a dog in the future and your dog may be destroyed. If you let your dog injure someone, you can be sent to prison for up to five years, or fined, or both.

As a decent human being, you also need to think of others. You know your dog and have a relationship with it, fine. But not everyone likes dogs, and some people have a real fear of dogs. Think about it from other people's perspective – a dog, big or small, running at you can be scary. Your dog should never be someone else's problem. Owners of other dogs might also have specific reasons that they do not want another dog racing over to theirs. This can range from a dog that is in training, to one that is injured or recovering from surgery, to one that has a contagious disease or is in season, to a nervous dog that is slowly learning to trust that it is safe on walks.

Finally, before we get into how to make that recall bombproof, I want to specifically mention two other examples that could cause serious problems if you don't have recall.

Assistance dogs and livestock

If your dog runs over to other dogs and you can't stop him, then you can't stop him running over to an assistance dog either. The assistance dog is there to provide crucial support to humans, some of whom rely on the dog to move around safely, and, if distracted by your dog, that could put that person in imminent danger and be life-threatening. It doesn't matter if your dog's intentions are friendly.

It's the same when it comes to livestock. Maybe your dog just wants to be friendly with the sheep, but farmers can legally shoot your dog if it is deemed a threat to their livestock, no questions asked, no benefit of doubt given. If you live in rural areas, with lots of livestock, you had better make sure your dog's recall is 110 per cent before unclipping that lead.

Now if it sounds like I'm being very negative and scare-mongering, understand it's because recall training is no joke and, as I said, can literally be the difference between life and death. You must make sure you have put in the work on this element of training and don't take chances.

HOW TO TEACH RECALL

First up, let's talk about where you should teach recall. Look to start in a quiet, non-distracting environment, like your own garden. Then build up to busier places, always using a long line, so you're never in a situation that puts your dog at risk.

I teach two types of recall: indirect recall and direct recall. And in both cases, we want to make sure that we are using a long line when we are teaching the two types of recall I use. I recommend a 30-foot (minimum) BioThane long line for this. These are tough leads but gentle on the hand and waterproof, so they're long-lasting and good all year round.

When teaching both types of recall we *always* begin with holding the long line and then progress to dropping it and letting the dog drag it around. This gives us a safety net should the dog fail. A foot on the long lead means you'll be able to stop your dog going off when it shouldn't.

Indirect recall

The best way to describe indirect recall would be when you say something along the lines of, 'Fido, this way'. This applies when your dog is wandering off and you just want it to come with you in your direction. Indirect recall means your dog doesn't have to come all the way to you, he just has to stay close and follow your direction. I teach this first because it makes that direct recall much easier.

To teach indirect recall I put the dog on a long line and when the dog wanders too far in front of me, I change direction and say, 'This way' and guide the dog back in my direction. I repeat the above many times, changing direction often.

The beauty of indirect recall is that you have probably been using this already on lead walks or over fields without even realising it, and, on the whole, it is easier for a lot of dogs to get. This one also means that the dog is paying more attention to you, because you are unpredictable when you keep changing direction. When a dog needs to pay attention to you, it's automatically listening to you too. This now makes it easier to teach direct recall.

I typically don't reward the indirect recall as the reward is that the dog is still technically free – he just has to follow you in your direction.

How To Train Your Dog

'Password: SDTBook'

Direct recall

This is probably the recall command you'll be expecting to use. Direct recall means, when you call 'Come', you expect your dog to come all the way to you and wait for a release from the command, rather than just carrying on in your general direction, doing whatever it was doing.

In the beginning, when your dog has returned to you at the 'Come' command, it's important to reward your dog every time, to drum home what you want. The reward could be a toy, food or fuss, or even just letting the dog go straight back out after coming back to you so the environment itself is the reward, if you have an avid sniffer. The main thing to remember is that if you use direct recall, you must make sure you release your dog afterwards.

At SDT we recommend practising both types of recall in conjunction with each other. This is because indirect recall means your dog is paying attention, and that's a great time to reinforce direct recall. Use both types of recall randomly for the best results rather than a week of one and then a week of the other.

If you're struggling here, try stripping it all back and ask yourself what the problem might be. Do you need to find a quieter place? Are you working too fast for your dog? Do you need to up your rewards or try something easier? Make your training sessions fun until motivation comes back.

NEXT STEPS

Once you've worked on your recall at home, in the garden or other places where you are free of distractions, you'll want to start to practise recall in many different areas. Start with places that have a low level of distractions – i.e., other dogs and people, strange sounds, smells and sights – and then build up to busier, more tempting areas. You need to practise recall within many different environments and it's a good idea to work through our socialising checklist on p.146 to get a rough idea of things you need to bombproof your dog around. You want to be confident that your dog can perform its recall 100 per cent of the time even when there are multiple tempting distractions.

As you progress in your recall teaching, you'll undoubtedly be faced with more and more challenges

– it's a necessary part of improving. But when you see distractions, don't panic! Here it's important we understand dogs and how they see things. Before your dog runs over to something, it will nearly always look back at you, especially if your foundations are there and you've been practising indirect recall. Often at this moment we panic and walk towards the dog to grab it, but the dog in this moment sees us moving in the direction they want to go and will often see this as a green light and run ahead. But, in fact, we need to move in the opposite direction.

When it comes to distractions, in the beginning I find 'This way' (indirect recall) works much better as you can have that lead and guide the dog back towards you, and in the opposite direction from the distraction. It's then easier to throw in a 'Come' command once the dog is moving towards you. This situation is a great opportunity to practise both types of recall.

TRAINING LEAD TIPS

You can stop holding the training lead when the dog is responding well to recall. This is also when I apply a little trick I like, which is to regularly step on the lead if the dog starts to stray too far. By doing this, it creates an invisible boundary and gets the dog paying more attention to you.

Another quick hack is if you have a powerful dog, tie some knots in the long line so it's easier to stop if the dog runs and you step on the lead. Bear in mind that any knots will shorten the lead length, so take that into account.

ARE ENCLOSED FIELDS GOOD?

I love enclosed fields for practising safe training, but a big mistake we make with these is letting the dog 100 per cent off lead when it's not fully trained. Although the field is safe and secure, if you find yourself having to repeat commands like 'Come' because the dog is not listening, there is a problem – and the field isn't helping. If your dog is ignoring you in a field when there are no distractions, what do you think will happen when you see a distraction away from the field? What is the dog learning? It is not learning to come when called, but instead that 'Come' often means you get to ignore your owner and do as you please (and self-reward with that freedom, thus giving even less incentive to do as asked).

Remember, if you want your dog to follow commands when something is going on that distracts them, then you must be consistent with your training when there is nothing going on too. Make sure you are still using your long line even in quiet areas or safe enclosed fields.

WHEN CAN I TRUST MY DOG OFF LEAD COMPLETELY?

The general rule is simple: you can let your dog off the lead once you've bombproofed it around as many distractions as possible – other animals, people, bikes, kites, birds, footballs and so on – *and* you've gone two weeks without having to step on that long line or pick it up in any way because the dog is listening to you. If this is seeming a way off, you could shorten the lead instead and keep shortening it until it's gone, but if you have to step on it or pick it up because the dog isn't responding to you when you give a command, you are not ready. Remember, long lines don't restrict freedom; they allow you to give freedom safely.

Recall training is a part of your daily life, indoors and out, so you must use a lead until you don't need it anymore.

TAKEAWAYS

- Recall is one of the most important commands you will ever teach your dog
- It is a mistake to let your dog off the lead too soon
- Letting dogs off the lead before they have hit the rebellious adolescent stage can also cause problems
- The dog owner with no recall is the worst type of owner because out-of-control dogs are a danger to themselves and others
- There is a legal requirement to control your dog, and an off-lead dog with no recall is out of control
- Failing to control your dog means that you could face a fine or imprisonment and your dog could be seized by the police, or legally shot by a farmer protecting livestock

- When teaching recall always use a long line, ideally a 30-foot (minimum) BioThane lead
- Indirect recall means your dog doesn't have to come all the way to you; he just has to stay close and follow your direction
- Direct recall is the use of the command 'Come', with your dog expected to come right to you and then wait to receive a release command
- Teaching and using indirect recall require the dog to focus his attention on you; this in turn helps with direct recall skills
- Once you have worked on your recall, start to practise recall in many different settings with all manner of distractions
- Enclosed fields are safe and secure but don't let your dog get away with not following commands when you are using them, because it will learn that ignoring you is okay
- You can let your dog off the lead once you've bombproofed him around distractions, but if he isn't responding to you when you give a command, you are not ready

Conclusion

So we've come to the end of the book guys, but for many the journey is just beginning. I want to leave you with some thoughts and, hopefully, words of wisdom!

As I mentioned earlier, there are so many gems to be found in rescue shelters. In fact, as I write this conclusion, I've literally just got myself another rescue dog, named Mila. She's a small terrier mix who was abandoned on the streets with her mum and littermates. When she was found, she was covered in mange and in a mess. Yet she's the most loving little dog you could meet. She knew nothing when I picked her up, but she was very friendly (as are most dogs in rescue), so if you are thinking of another dog, please do consider adopting – there are so many lovely dogs there needing homes.

Whether you have a rescue, a new puppy, or an older dog (or more!), if you are using this book for the dog/s you already have or because you are adding another to your household, please understand that dog training is a journey. It's about building a relationship and it's about enjoying the process. You don't need to achieve everything on day one. You don't need to be hard on yourself if it doesn't always go to plan. You are not in competition with anyone. You don't have to prove anything to anyone. The only person you have to answer to is yourself, and the only thing that matters is you and your family (if you are close to them) and your dog.

Dog training is about the fun times and the bad times, and if you are trying your best that's all that matters. Remember guys, I'm starting this journey all over again myself so I'm right there with you. This book has come at the perfect time for me, but also, hopefully, at the right time for you guys too.

I want to thank everyone who follows us on social media and everyone who is a member of our online group. I want to thank those who have booked sessions with us, past and present, and everyone who has bought our last book and this one too. It's because of you guys I'm here today writing this book and helping you and many others.

So thank you, and I love you,

Adam

Stay in touch:

Let us know how your training has gone at:

YouTube @southenddogtraining1

Facebook https://www.facebook.com/southenddogtrainingandwalking/

Instagram @southenddogtraining

TikTok @ southenddogtraining1

Twitter @_sdtofficial

Daily journal Date:

Today's rating: ☆ ☆ ☆ ☆ ☆

Today's training goal:

How do I feel?

....

....

....

....

....

....

....

....

Today's wins:

....
....
....
....
....
....
....
....

What can I do better tomorrow?

....
....
....
....
....
....
....
....

What did I learn?

Index